An Introduction to the
Russian Mennonites

An Introduction to the
Russian Mennonites

Wally Kroeker

Good Books

Intercourse, PA 17534
800/762-7171
www.goodbks.com

To the memory of
Madeline Kroeker and Mary Loewen,
my mother and mother-in-law,
who sought to carry with dignity and grace
the scars of their Russian uprooting.

Credits and Acknowledgments

Photographs from the Provincial Archives of Manitoba, top photo on cover and 40; by William Schroeder, center photo on cover; by Wally Kroeker, inset photo on cover, 6, 11, 14, 15, 18, 20, 21, 31, 35, 36, 45, 56, 57, 58, 70, 75, 76, 80, 82, 83, 85, 93, 95, 96, 98, 99 (both), 104, 107, 108, 110, 111; by Peter Gerhard Rempel, bottom photo on cover; from Centre for Mennonite Brethren Studies, 9 (#NP12-01-271), 24 (#NP108-08-211), 25 (#NP006-01-0022), 28 (#NP108-01-0061), 29 (#NP108-08-0071), 32 (#NP108-08-0191), 59 (top #NP080-01-031), 60 (top #NP15-01-341, bottom #NP080-01-021), 61 (top #NP15-01-351, bottom #NP07-01-071), 62 (#NP015-01-01); from Mennonite Heritage Centre Photograph Collection, 17 (#505-83), 26 (#a61-31), 27 (#a61-41), 43 (#285-143), 44 (#578-101), 46 (#a61-351), 47 (#a62-181), 59 (bottom left #a62-221, bottom right #a62-201); by A.A. Kroeker, 71, 74; by Jake Epp, 91; from MEDA, 101; by Agnes DeFehr, 121.

Maps created by Ray Dirks.

Excerpt from *Through Fire & Water: An Overview of Mennonite History* by Harry Loewen and Steven Nolt, found on p. 33, is used by permission of Herald Press.

The author also wishes to thank several people who helped along the way: Conrad Stoesz (CMBS), Alf Redekopp (MHC), Abe Dueck, Harold Jantz, Paul Toews, and Rudy Friesen.

The bottom cover photo depicts a celebration on the grounds of the Chortitza Mennonite Church (shown in background). The young women in white uniforms are students at the nearby Mennonite Maedchenschule (girls school), which is pictured on page 31. The photo was taken by prominent Russian Mennonite photographer Peter Gerhard Rempel, who is referred to on pages 27-28 of this book. Photo used by permission of John Rempel.

Design by Dawn J. Ranck

AN INTRODUCTION TO THE RUSSIAN MENNONITES
Copyright © 2005 by Good Books, Intercourse, PA 17534
International Standard Book Number: 1-56148-391-5
Library of Congress Catalog Card Number: 2005000311

Library of Congress Cataloging-in-Publication Data
Kroeker, Wally
  An introduction to the Russian Mennonites / Wally Kroeker.
    p. cm.
  ISBN 1-56148-391-5 (pbk.)
  1. Mennonites--Russia--History. 2. Mennonites--North America--History.
I. Title.
  BX8119.R8K76 2005
  289.7'47--dc22   2005000311

Table of Contents

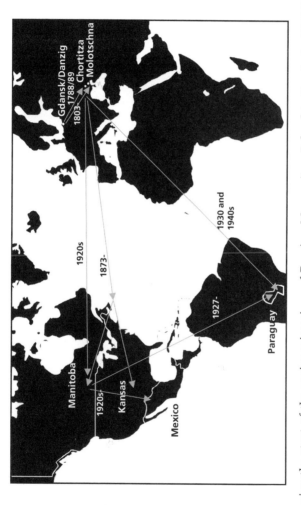

Map showing the start of the major migrations of Russian Mennonites: Poland to Russia in 1788/89 and 1803; Russia to Kansas and Manitoba in 1873; Russia to Canada in the 1920s; Canada to Mexico and Paraguay in the 1920s; and Russia to South America in the 1930s and 40s.

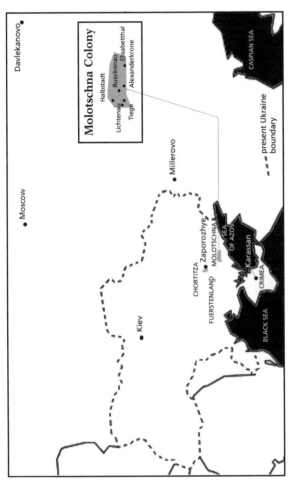

Map of western Russia showing some of the major Mennonite colonies and place names mentioned in this book. The inset map at right shows locations in the Molotschna Colony. The broken-line border indicates present-day Ukraine, which now encompasses much of the area occupied by Mennonites in the 1800s and 1900s.

Introduction

Travel the plains of Kansas in late spring and you will see plenty of wheat. The fields are a wall-to-wall carpet of natural green, laid down by human hands and the forces of nature. Growing there is a special kind of wheat, with hard, protein-rich kernels that make top-quality flour for the best grade of bread.

Kansas Mennonites will be happy to explain how this particular variety of wheat came to mid-America. They will tell you about Anna Barkman, the young immigrant girl who carefully sewed her rag doll full of the hearty kernels before leaving Russia in 1874. They will tell you how those few handfuls of grain became the seed of new life for the first Russian Mennonites who came to North America.

Travel north out of Kansas through Nebraska, the Dakotas, and finally into Manitoba, and you can follow the harvest as it rolls like falling dominoes over the plains. In Manitoba, too, a sturdy agricultural foundation was laid down by Russian Mennonites who came in the 1870s and transformed the prairie into their own version of Eden.

This is their story. It is, first of all, a story of faith, of Anabaptist faith that could not be suppressed. It is also a human story, with cultural and economic dimensions that make the Russian Mennonites unique.

1.
How They Got
to Russia

If you visit long enough with Mennonites in places like Kansas or Manitoba, you will eventually hear the term "Russian Mennonite." That may sound odd, as the people you're talking with may be third- or fourth-generation North Americans and may never have been anywhere close to Russia.

What you're hearing distinguishes this type of Mennonite from what are sometimes called "Swiss-German Mennonites"—an earlier immigrant group who populated Pennsylvania, Virginia, and other places in the eastern parts of North America. The Russian Mennonites (a more accurate term might be Dutch-Russian Mennonites) have last names like Wiebe, Penner, and Friesen and enjoy their own traditional foods like *zwieback* (double-decker buns) and *borscht* (cabbage soup). Their ancestors likely spoke *Plattdeutsch* (Low German) at home. You may also pick up slight peculiarities in temperament, in how they worship, and in how they interact with the government and the wider culture (more about that later).

For now, let's just understand that these people descend from north European Mennonites who found their

A field of sunflowers, a prominent "Mennonite crop," in the former colony of Fuerstenland.

way to Russia in the late 1700s, established their own Mennonite "commonwealth" there and began emigrating to North America in the 1870s.

But how did they get to the vast steppes of Russia in the first place?

Looking for refuge

The 16th century was tough on a new breed of Christians who emerged in Switzerland and Holland during what is called the Radical Reformation. These people believed baptism should be a voluntary step for adult Christians, not something to be forced upon a helpless infant. In 1525 they broke away from the established church and began to practice a voluntary second baptism, and thus were dubbed Anabaptists. Gradually they came to be known as Mennonites, after Menno Simons, a former priest around whose leadership the young movement coalesced.

The Mennonites soon became a spiritual force to be reckoned with across northern Europe. Their new faith, based on an adult choice to become part of the church, was a threat to ecclesiastical leaders who were accustomed to wielding unfettered control with no argument. The authorities took unkindly to these disobedient upstarts, chasing them from one place to another, burning some and drowning others. Those who survived sought refuge wherever they could. Throughout their history, their beliefs, especially their belief that Christians should have no part in making war, made them a people on the move.

In those days, Europe wasn't yet divided into countries as it is today. It had numerous smaller regions governed by princes and other rulers, some of whom were quite strict about the kind of religious beliefs people should have.

Others were more relaxed about religious beliefs, or had more pressing issues to deal with. One such region could be described as Polish-Prussia, known today as Poland. Its ruling princes, as well as the later King Frederick the Great (1740-86), provided a haven of refuge. They had ulterior motives for welcoming the persecuted Mennonites. For one thing, a flow of new immigrants would replace huge numbers who had been wiped out by the plague. For another, they needed help with water.

Back in Holland the Mennonites had learned a few things about water and how to control it. Now they would find a new outlet for those skills. Polish-Prussia needed land reclaimed from the delta of the Vistula River. The Mennonites flocked there, first of all to Danzig (known today as Gdansk) and then to other areas. They built dikes and reclaimed rich farmland from what had previously been swamps and mud.

In return for their diligent work the newcomers were offered religious tolerance, exemption from military service, and room to grow.

A place to call home

The Mennonites went to work, carving out a new way of living—together, and out of harm's way. Maybe here they would finally find peace. They formed villages of a couple of dozen families. Besides their farmland, each family had a large garden as well as a few cows and pigs. While they enjoyed being able to keep to themselves, they were open to others who found their faith and lifestyle attractive, people with Polish names like Sawatsky, Rogalsky, and Pankratz.

The Lutheran church leaders, who dominated the town councils, weren't fond of the Mennonites. They were jealous of how the resilient newcomers could rebound from any setback and flourish wherever they were planted. After Frederick the Great died in 1786, pressure on the Mennonites grew. Special taxes were levied, some of which went to support the military. Restrictive laws were passed to keep them from buying land, which meant growing families couldn't expand their farms.

Farming was still the Mennonites' dominant livelihood, but many were merchants, weavers, and artisans. Even they felt the press of restrictions. Mennonites were prevented from joining professional guilds. Thus the art of clockmaking, for example, at which Mennonites excelled, became an underground industry.

Once again, the Mennonites felt pressure from a combination of political, economic, and religious forces. While not openly persecuted, they were clearly second-class citizens. And things would likely get worse. Europe was in upheaval as a result of the French Revolution. As nervous regions bolstered their defenses, Mennonite leaders and parents wondered how long their young men would be spared from military involvement.

Many started looking northward to the huge new frontier of Russia, where Czarina Catherine the Great was opening wide her arms to foreigners of many stripes.

And once again . . .

Russia's ruler was not just being benevolent. She needed resourceful settlers to come and put down roots and solidify her claim to the Ukraine, which she had seized from the Turkish army in the Russo-Turkish War (1781-92). She offered the Mennonites (and other groups) a tempting deal. They would have large areas all to them-

A new homeland in Russia gave Mennonites a place to work, worship, and raise families without being disturbed. Many built homes like this one in Rosental, Chortitza Colony.

selves. They could worship freely, run their own form of local government, and operate their own schools in the German language. Best of all, their young men would never have to serve in the military.

When a Russian colonization agent came to Danzig to make his sales pitch to the Mennonites, it sounded too good to be true. They wanted to assess the situation for themselves.

In 1786 Jacob Hoeppner and Johann Bartsch, like the spies sent out by Joshua of the Old Testament, went to Russia to scout the land. After a year's investigation they came back with a glowing report.

In 1788 a group of eight families left Polish-Prussia by foot and wagon for what they hoped would be the new promised land for the Mennonites. The next year they were followed by several hundred families. Imagine their disappointment when they found terrain studded with rocks and pocked with gullies. Where was the ground they had been promised?

The Russians' excuse was that the land had since been overrun by Turks and was no longer safe. Were they telling the truth? Or was this an early version of bait-and-switch?

In any case, the Mennonites were now there and began to occupy what became known as the Chortitza Colony. (It would also be referred to as the Old Colony, because it was established first.) Later on, the Russians offered better land for the second large colony, Molotschna. These were not colonies in the traditional sense of small communities. These were huge tracts of land—Chortitza was over 100,000 acres and Molotschna three times that size. In time, many smaller colonies were added, bringing the Mennonites' total area to several million acres.

A remaining "Mennonite house" in the former Molotschna Colony, occupied today by Ukrainians.

Promises to keep

Catherine made good on her offer. She drew up a charter of privileges in 1788 (which were later reaffirmed by her son, Czar Paul), providing a tangible written guarantee of all the things promised to lure the Mennonites from Polish-Prussia. Praising the newcomers for their "excellent industry and morality," and setting them up as "a model to the foreigners," the document gave the Mennonites sweeping economic, religious, and legal privileges.

Each family was given, free of charge, 65 *desiatini* of land (175 acres). The Mennonites could use this land to farm and develop whatever economic structures they needed, including factories. They received farm and business loans, as well as a 10-year tax holiday. The government promised complete liberty in internal religious matters but insisted they not proselytize their non-Mennonite neighbors. Mennonites did not have to enter the military, and in legal matters they were allowed to affirm

rather than swear oaths (which was the Mennonite pref-
erence, based on Matthew 5:33-37). While subject to the
national government in larger matters, they were given
jurisdiction over education and local administration within their colonies. They were like a state within the state.

They were promised that the Russian authorities
would leave them "in unmolested enjoyment of their
houses, lands, and other possessions, not to hinder them
in the enjoyment of the privileges granted to them . . . ."

This was music to Mennonite ears. At last they would
have what they had hoped for in Prussia—a place where
they could work and worship freely, a place to safeguard
their faith and way of life. Some even saw Catherine's in-
vitation as divine providence.

Back in Polish-Prussia, more and more Mennonites
piled their wagons high with household goods and farm
implements and took to the road.

The Mennonites were on the move.

2.
Building the Mennonite Colonies

Getting 175 acres of land—free—was a major incentive to resettle in Russia. But it had to be earned.

The new land was wild and untamed. It wasn't as fertile as the Mennonites were used to, rain wasn't as regular or plentiful, and there were new pests to deal with, like infestations of grasshoppers. The Mennonites' first homes—dugouts and sod huts—were literally clawed out of the soil.

But the people adapted and did exactly what the Russians had hoped. They picked up their tools and went to work. They coaxed forth one crop and then another, improving the land and the yield with each succeeding year, eventually transforming the unsparing landscape into vistas of lush grain. The government was delighted. It needed farm commodities to meet larger international commitments. And with the Mennonites and other groups of newcomers fully settled in, the Russian claim to the land was now beyond dispute.

The flow of Mennonites from Polish-Prussia continued. The next wave of immigrants included more educated and entrepreneurial folk who initially may have felt they had too much at stake in Polish-Prussia to give it up. When they arrived, progress accelerated.

The Mennonites put their hands to replicating the village pattern they had found so appealing in Polish-Prussia. They divided themselves into villages of 15 to 30 families. In a gesture of nostalgia or historic respect, they named some of their communities after those they left behind—Halbstadt, Rosenort, and Ohrloff.

Each village elected its own *schulze* (mayor). At the top of the colony's administrative structure was an *oberschulze* (district chairman), who also served as a liaison with the Russian officials in Odessa. Most internal ad-

A windmill in the former village of Alexanderkrone. Last used in 1952, it is the only Mennonite windmill left in the former Russian Mennonite colonies.

Petershagen Mennonite Church, Molotschna Colony. Built in 1892, it had 350 members and four ministers by 1909. During the Soviet era, it was used for storage. It has recently been restored by a group of Canadian Mennonites and is again being used today as a Mennonite meetinghouse.

ministrative matters, such as taxes and finances, were left in Mennonite hands.

Each village had a central street lined with homesteads. In the center of the village was a school and perhaps a church. As they had in Prussia, the colonists built new homes with house and barn connected so one could take care of chores without venturing out into the bitter cold. Land was parceled out in pieces so that everyone shared equally in the quality of the soil.

Eventually, Chortitza would have 18 villages, and the larger Molotschna Colony, roughly a hundred miles southeast, 58. When additional colonies were established, the number of Mennonite villages in Russia reached several hundred.

Village life was simple with virtually no outside amusements. During the week, life consisted mainly of work, and everyone got involved. Mixed farms had plenty of chores. The fields of grain needed tending. The animals needed to be pastured and fed. Eggs had to be gathered. Produce was preserved to last through the winter. There was always something to do.

It was here where many of the Russian Mennonites' distinctive foods became part of their tradition. (More about this in Chapter 8.) Some foods grew out of the need to make do with very little. Time-worn recipe collections contain procedures for making foods like "water soup," a concoction of water, slab bacon, and an onion, to which simple flour dumplings are added. The popular "summer borscht" is one of countless soups made with a ham bone, onions, and potatoes and flavored with readily available herbs like sorrel.

There is speculation that *zwieback*, the legendary double-decker buns for which Russian Mennonites are famous, originated during this time in the Mennonite wanderings. The word *zwieback* (literally "two-bake" in Low German) is not the double roasted item of German fame but a bun of two rolls perched one atop the other. As one traditional recipe book notes, "Wherever our people settled, they grew wheat. No wonder our mothers and grandmothers were experts at baking breads and *zwieback*. No one had to go hungry when there was bread in the house . . . ." The buns are made of dough similar to bread but a bit saltier and richer in butter. In most Russian Mennonite homes, *zwieback* were baked on Saturday to reduce the amount of labor needed on Sunday.

Another staple of Mennonite farm life was the pig. Butchering ranked just behind Christmas and Easter as a memorable time of year. Several families often got together for this fall ritual. The men killed and butchered the animals, and the womenfolk cleaned the meat and

Once Mennonites had tamed the soil, they began erecting factories to produce bricks, tiles, and farm implements. Some can be seen in this early photo of the Chortitza skyline.

rendered the lard, which in farm families of the day took the place of butter. Hams and sides of bacon were smoked. The intestines were cleaned and used as casings for liver and pork sausage. The pig's feet, knuckles, heart, tongue, ears, and some of the rind were used to make head cheese. It was often said that the Mennonites used every part of the pig but the squeal.

Down on the farm

To no one's surprise, the Mennonites soon distinguished themselves as farmers. Agriculture took a giant leap forward, thanks to Johann Cornies (1789-1848), a brilliant farmer and agricultural statesman whose reputation eventually extended to the far reaches of the Russian empire. He encouraged diversification into sheep and cattle breeding, as well as growing new crops such as flax, potatoes, and various fruits. Others took note of his suc-

The Heinrich Schroeder company in Halbstadt, Molotschna Colony, sold and serviced pumps, plows, and threshing machines in the early 1900s. The building is still in use today.

cessful experiments with mulberry trees and silkworms, leading to a flourishing silk industry. The Mennonites in Russia became widely known as much for their farming practices as for their religious identity.

Despite his achievements, Cornies would eventually become too powerful for some tastes. While some saw him in positive terms, like a Mennonite Johnny Appleseed, others saw him as a Mennonite czar.

Agribusinesses arose to meet new opportunities, not only at home but farther afield. Every village had its own flour mill, rudimentary at first, but later quite modern. Mennonites became known for their excellent milling practices. Some Mennonite millers became exceedingly prosperous. One eventually won a gold medal at the world's fair in Paris for the quality of his flour.

Factories were established to produce farm implements such as plows, mowers, even sophisticated reapers, and threshing machines. Brick and tile production developed as the increasingly affluent Mennonites turned to masonry—and, in turn, new architectural styles—to succeed the clapboard buildings that had in their day replaced the early sod huts. Markets for these products were found beyond the boundaries of the colonies, providing new streams of income. Not only had the Mennonites fashioned a self-sufficient economy, they had also found ways to bring in revenue from the outside.

Mennonites were becoming increasingly comfortable. Never before—not in Holland, not in Polish-Prussia—had they been able to live and farm with this amount of freedom. But they couldn't sit still. There was always a need for more land to accommodate the large families. Since farms couldn't be subdivided under Russian law, a growing landless group emerged.

Hub of village life

Mennonites consciously carried their faith with them, wherever they went. The outward trappings of this faith were remarkably consistent throughout the Mennonite world. The church was central to village life—in more ways than one. Several villages came together for worship.

In the early days, a typical meetinghouse was a rectangular wooden structure with a platform along one side for the pulpit and a bench for the *vorsaenger* (literally, foresingers), who were an important feature of the worship service. They intoned the lines of each hymn (slowly, even laboriously) ahead of the congregation. No musical instruments were used. The people sat in long backless benches, men and women on separate sides of the congregation. (An excellent example of this architecture can be found in the Mennonite Heritage Village in southern

Manitoba.) Later on, church buildings became more elaborate as architectural styles were adapted from Europe.

There were no paid, full-time church leaders. At first ministers were farmers and later teachers who were chosen from among the membership for their spiritual and leadership qualities. Some were set aside for even higher responsibility as *aelteste* (elders), similar to the role of bishop.

Muddying the waters

The seeds were also sown for another factor that would loom large in later years. Since Russia had offered special privileges to the Mennonites, and these Mennonites were now in charge of their own local governance, church membership became intertwined with civic iden-

The Halbstadt Zentralschule (central school) in Russia was a secondary school for boys and later added a program to train teachers. Built in 1895, it was the only building in the Mennonite colonies to utilize Greek columns. After the Mennonite exodus, the building was occupied for many years by the regional Communist Party.

The former Mennonite girls' school was built in Halbstadt (since renamed Molochansk), Russia, in 1882. It has recently been refurbished to serve as a Mennonite Center offering spiritual and humanitarian aid to local Ukrainian residents.

tity. One needed to be a Mennonite in order to enjoy the special Mennonite privileges. How did one become a Mennonite? By joining the church. Everyone eventually joined, seemingly regardless of spiritual commitment. Some merely wanted the rights of citizenship.

It was not always clear whether the colony leaders were religious or civil leaders. Some Mennonites felt that their leaders were more intent on preserving the status quo than in nourishing a vibrant faith.

As a result, the idea of Mennonite identity became murky. As Frank H. Epp wrote, "It was in Russia that the ethnic quality of being a Mennonite became mixed and sometimes confused with the religious quality" (1974, p. 164).

Meanwhile, the Mennonites kept coming, off and on, for more than 50 years. Some emigrated from Polish-Prussia as entire congregations. Their number in Russia reached 35,000 by the 1850s; according to some sources, the total Mennonite population of the colonies plus Siberia and other parts of Russia grew to 120,000 by the end of World War I. None of the growth came as the result of outreach. The Russian Orthodox Church, anxious to retain its power, exerted considerable pressure to make sure the Mennonites did not proselytize their neighbors. As C. Henry Smith noted, "The growth of the church in Russia was rather a swarming of the people than an expansion of a faith" (1950, p. 469).

3.
The Golden Age in Russia

By the beginning of the 20th century, the Mennonites of Russia had developed organizationally and prospered significantly. Their villages were picture-book scenes of freshly painted brick buildings, magnificent flower gardens, and lush orchards surrounded by bountiful crops. Their training facilities and welfare institutions were a matter of pride. They had orphanages, old folks homes, a mental hospital, and a school for the deaf and mute.

Their bustling businesses (agribusiness, milling, clockmaking) made them known across the country. Despite being largely a farming people, the Mennonites built numerous factories which accounted for six percent of the country's industrial output. Some of the factories employed hundreds of people and produced up to 3,000 implements a year. Czars and foreign dignitaries visited the colonies to behold this immigrant success story and perhaps to note how much further they had progressed than their Slavic neighbors.

Historian Frank H. Epp said the Mennonite colonies "had become the most prosperous and well-developed rural communities in all of Russia" (1962, p. 27).

Neighbors pitch in to help raise this barn after a fire in Rueckenau, Russia, 1904.

While many Mennonites lived in quaint villages, the pulse of their business and industry was decidedly urban. In economic matters, Mennonites had succeeded enormously.

They had achieved great wealth and influence. When threats of creeping nationalism frightened some 18,000 Mennonites into moving to North America between 1874 and 1880, their vacant farms, often sold at bargain prices to those who chose to stay, enabled some to augment their wealth. Other wealthy farmers continued to invest in land outside the colonies; hundreds of farms became major estates. Several landowners had 50,000 acres, a few 100,000 acres, and one had more than 200,000 acres.

Mennonites traveled regularly to the citadels of power. Some were elected to leading national positions in agriculture and industry. One was mayor of Ekaterinoslav (today Dnieperpetrosk) for several years. In the early 1900s, two became members of the Imperial Duma (Russian Parliament).

Education catches up

Culturally, the Mennonites took more time to reach their stride. The field of education was slow to gain traction. Upon arriving in Russia, they set up an elementary school in each village, but the quality of education at the outset was not high. The teaching was basic and sometimes went little beyond memorization of Scripture. Teachers weren't well trained or well paid. For a while it seemed that the purpose of education was mainly to perpetuate the faith and the German language.

But with time this changed. Teaching became a respected profession, second only to farming. By 1914, according to one tally, the Mennonites in Russia boasted several hundred elementary schools, more than a dozen high schools, and several girls' schools, as well as teachers' colleges, trade schools, and a business college. Many

Teaching became a respected profession once the Mennonites gained a vision for education. A prominent teacher was Aron P. Toews, shown in the center of this end-of-school-year photo of students at Rueckenau school in Russia in 1911.

promising students were sent to Russian universities and even to universities and seminaries in Europe.

As commitment to education grew, so did the Mennonites' literary interest. Like education, publishing was slow to develop, due in part to the restrictive Russian environment. It was simpler to import reading material from Europe. Other than songbooks, little Mennonite publishing took place in 19th-century Russia.

Toward the end of the century, publishing began to gather steam. The Raduga (Rainbow) Press started to publish devotional materials in 1897 and in 1903 launched *Friedensstimme*, the first Mennonite periodical in Russia.

Great educational strides were made during the Mennonite Golden Era. A variety of elementary and secondary schools, teachers' colleges, trade schools, and a business college were established. There was even a school for the deaf. In this photo of the Tiege school in Russia, instructor Henry Peters teaches a class of hearing-impaired young people.

Instructor Abram Wiebe teaches students to form sounds at a school for the deaf in Tiege, Russia.

It would eventually reach a circulation of 5,800. Other initiatives included *The Mennonite Brotherhood in Russia, 1789-1910* by Peter Martin Friesen. Raduga became a leading publisher of evangelical literature for groups beyond the Mennonites. In 1912, a teacher by the name of Peter Harder authored *Die Lutherische Cousine*, the first novel written by a Russian Mennonite.

A taste of finery

No longer did Mennonites feel isolated in their villages and colonies. New cultural vistas beckoned. Mennonites, more world-wise if not worldly, became less modest about adopting the styles and indulgences of the day.

Peter Gerhard Rempel (1872-1933), a professional studio photographer, captured the courtly yearnings, and

Mennonite prosperity began to show during the "Golden Era." This photo is of the Franz Martens yard in Molotschna Colony, taken around 1900.

perhaps even the pretensions, of many Mennonites during the Golden Age before World War I. A journey through his extant work depicts Mennonites posing stiffly (as was the custom) with a landed gentry elegance that clashes with the rustic myth of settler life. The time-frozen tableaux convey a willing embrace of something larger than the colony consciousness.

"While individuals posed seriously and solemnly . . . against his [Rempel's] imported backdrops, they were making gestures affirming unspoken sentiments and conventions," say the authors of *Forever Summer, Forever Sunday*, a published collection of Rempel's work. They suggest "a collective wish of the Mennonites of Russia to project an image of themselves as individuals who had come to adopt comfortably the conventional manners and dress of European society."

Fissures start to form

On the religious front, not all was quiet. Although the Mennonites seemed like a united group, their garment was not without seams. From the start, the immigrants had brought with them the differences that existed between them in Polish-Prussia. There were differences in temperament and lifestyle, as well as strongly divergent views on spiritual leadership and congregational discipline. Some of the differences hardened into rifts.

The first religious split occurred in 1814. A small group had been meeting separately since 1812 because they felt spiritual life in the larger church was at a low ebb. Some of the specific concerns were lack of personal morality and ethics, Mennonite financial support of Russian militarism, and the use of corporal punishment by some Mennonite civic leaders. This group was derisively called the *Kleine Gemeinde* (small church), a name which the

A school outing of the Karassan high school in Crimea in 1901.

breakaway group eventually used for itself. Today its descendants exist in Canada as the Evangelical Mennonite Conference and in Latin America as the continuing *Kleine Gemeinde.*

A larger, more acrimonious schism occurred in 1860. Influenced strongly by pietist Lutheran preachers from Germany and earlier Moravian exposures, a group of 18 dissident Mennonites rebelled against what they regarded as spiritual decay in the mother church and began holding communion separately. In the warmth of their newly articulated spirituality, the men addressed one another as "brother"; hence they became known as the Mennonite Brethren Church. In contrast to other Mennonite groups who baptized by sprinkling or pouring, the Mennonite Brethren chose to baptize by fully immersing candidates backwards in water to symbolize the death and resurrection of Christ.

This defection proved to be much more disruptive than the earlier split. How should the mother church deal with this "new sect," as some defined them? The colony leaders wanted to see the dissidents either return to the larger church or be stripped of their privileges. Eventually the Mennonite Brethren appealed to the Russian authorities and were given official recognition as Mennonites. The tensions around this difficult beginning generated great bitterness. Some of the dissidents were imprisoned and whipped. Sanity eventually returned, but harsh feelings prevailed, in some cases for generations.

A third, smaller group emerged in 1905. It was called the *Allianz Gemeinde* (alliance church) because it sought to heal earlier rifts. It was tolerant when it came to baptism, accepting modes of immersion, pouring, or sprinkling. It faded from view when its members migrated to North America and joined Mennonite Brethren churches.

The Mennonite Maedchenschule (girls school) in Chortitza.
Built in 1895, it is still used as a school in present-day Ukraine.

These splits do not suggest there was no vitality in the mother church, sometimes described with the term *Kirchliche*, or church Mennonites. There were those in the existing church who longed for heightened spiritual fervor but did not feel withdrawal was the way to achieve it. Perhaps stimulated by the wake-up call of the Mennonite Brethren defection, they worked even harder for higher standards of education and promoted missions and outreach.

Beginning in 1871, *Kirchliche* Mennonites sent missionaries to Java, Sumatra, and Egypt. The new Mennonite Brethren group sent workers to India and Africa beginning in 1889. Prominent preachers and teachers from Europe visited the colonies, speaking at places like the month-long Apanlee Bible conferences hosted at the sprawling grounds of the wealthy estate owner David Dick.

Among the new cultural benefits of rising prosperity was professional photography. Many family albums featured formal images like this 1915 photograph of teachers and their wives before principal F. C. Thiessen and Jacob Toews at the school in Dawlekanowo, Ufa, Russia.

While Mennonites had become more world-wise, they managed to hold on to some key faith tenets, such as nonresistance. In World War I, 13,000 Mennonite men were mobilized for service in the Red Cross or other kinds of nonmilitary service like forestry. Only a very few served in the army.

Storm clouds ahead

For those who owned land or factories, life during the Mennonite Golden Age was thoroughly satisfying. But not everyone could own land.

The Mennonites had large families, and Russian rules didn't allow the original holdings to be subdivided. By the mid-1800s, the population of the colonies had swelled to 35,000, and by the end of World War I to 120,000. There wasn't enough farmland for everyone.

A subgroup of landless Mennonites emerged. Since voting was based on land ownership, they were a people without influence or status, destined for a life as employees doing mundane tasks for others. They were often exploited. In some cases they were charged exorbitant fees to use community pastureland. As this landless class grew, eventually composing half of the Mennonite population, discontent rose. At one point the Russian government stepped in to arrange the subdivision of some communal land. This provided a measure of relief, but the ongoing economic discontent frayed the community fabric.

On the religious front, the self-government that seemed like such a blessing at first began to show itself as a two-edged sword. Mennonite civil authorities often ran into conflict with church leaders. Historians would later call what emerged a Mennonite state or commonwealth.

"In Russia, Mennonite faith and ethnicity became almost identical. It was nearly impossible to separate culture, social life, and religious faith. To get married or hold office in a Mennonite colony, one had to receive baptism and belong to the church. A Russian Mennonite was a member of an ethnic group. Thus Mennonite peoplehood, begun in Prussia, was confirmed and further developed in Russia. The Russian government considered Mennonites an ethnic group, distinct from all other German settlers. Sometimes being Mennonite had little to do with faith and a Christian life" (Loewen and Nolt 1996, p. 219).

Russia had done well by these immigrants. Left to themselves, the overachieving Mennonites had held up their side of the bargain, contributing enormously to the economic fabric of the nation. But their immediate neighbors were jealous. It didn't help that the Mennonites could seem to be self-righteous and that they were not immune to prejudice. Many considered the Russian peasantry to be inferior and sometimes let it show.

And if that wasn't enough, the Mennonites wouldn't "do their duty" by going to war when others were called.

The Test of Time

When the Great Trek from Russia began in the 1870s, hundreds of Mennonites lugged a particularly precious cargo – a wall clock with bulky pendulum and heavy brass weights. Many were secured in wooden hope chests or wicker baskets. Some were swaddled in blankets on laps, never out of sight until they reached their new home on the frontier plains of Kansas or Manitoba.

Of all the output generated by Mennonite business activity in Russia, the clock stands out as an economic artifact, marking much more than the strides of time.

Who were the craftsmen who put a clock in every home? Theirs were names like Lepp, Hamm, Mandtler, and Hildebrand. But the one that started it all and endured the longest was Kroeger. Today, decades after the Kroeger company closed its doors, Russian Mennonite clocks are prized as heirlooms and sought after by collectors.

Locate one in a Mennonite museum and you will be struck by its primitive simplicity—a large metal

A no-frills Kroeger clock, highly prized by collectors today.

wall clock with a long brass pendulum, driven by brass weights on a string. No frills; no fancy cabinet nor glass case. Just a well-crafted clock for simple Mennonite farmsteads of the 18th and 19th centuries. Plenty good for folk who measured life in seasons rather than hours.

The skill of clockmaking grew out of blacksmithing. Clockmakers, who had to know mathematics, metallurgy, and precision engineering, were the master mechanics of their time.

Mennonite clockmaking dates back almost to the beginning of the Anabaptist movement. Hutterites made clocks for church towers as early as 1572. By the 1700s, a dynasty of Mennonite clockmakers had grown up in southwest Germany. These skills were dispersed as the Mennonites migrated—some to the eastern U.S. and others to the new colonies in Russia.

When Johann Kroeger migrated to the Chortitza Colony in the early 1800s, he became the first Mennonite clockmaker in Russia. For four generations thereafter, the Kroegers made long pendulum wall clocks. Others, like Lepp, Hamm, and Hildebrand, came later and lasted only one generation.

For a time, Mennonite clockmaking in the Danzig area of Polish-Prussia had been an underground industry. Guilds of major trades did not permit newcomers

Arthur Kroeger displays one of many historic Russian clocks he has restored.

to work, especially if they were despised Anabaptists. Only guild members were allowed to mark their products with their names. When the Kroeger clockmakers moved to Russia, they continued the tradition of not marking their clocks, though there were some exceptions.

"If a Russian clock has no markings at all, it most likely is a Kroeger," says Arthur Kroeger of Winnipeg, a descendant of the clockmaking clan.

A native of Russia who emigrated to Canada via Germany in 1949, Kroeger has distinguished himself as a restorer of clocks. Clocks are not only his rewarding hobby but also a treasured link with his past. As with many Russian Mennonites, his past is filled with tragedy. The Kroeger family suffered greatly under the Bolsheviks. Kroeger's grandfather David, the last Kroeger to make a living at clocks, was beaten to death by anarchists.

In 1990 a clock came into Kroeger's Winnipeg shop for repair. When he examined the mechanism, he made a startling discovery. Inside were scratched the initials of his father, who would have been 16, possibly still an apprentice, when he worked on that particular clock. He died in a Soviet concentration camp in 1942.

What helped spell the end of the Kroeger clock dynasty was the product's simple sturdiness.

"They made their clocks too good," says Kroeger of his forebears. "The market became saturated, and there was no obsolescence."

The start of the electric era finished off the mechanical clock business, says Kroeger.

He thinks his forebears might have prolonged the life of their company by adapting to the times and diversifying into different models with fancy cases. But they were Mennonites who still valued simplicity.

"They had a fear of becoming too worldly," he says.

Kroeger's research suggests that Mennonite clockmakers in Russia manufactured some 10,000 to 12,000 clocks in a 100-year period. About 80 percent of them were made by Kroegers.

Kroeger estimates there still are a couple of hundred clocks in homes in Canada, the U.S., and Central and South Americas. They have become collectors' items and can fetch high prices.

With the possible exception of the family hope chest, the clock was the leading Mennonite export from Russia. For Mennonite immigrants enduring poverty and hardship in their new land, the reassuring ticking of a Mennonite clock was the sound of a mechanical heartbeat connecting them with their past.

4.
The Great Treks

They started leaving in the 1870s, from the steppes of Russia to the central plains of the United States and Canada. Once again they collected what they couldn't do without, traveled by beast and wagon to seagoing vessels, crossed the stormy Atlantic, and went on by train to sodbuster homesteads on the frontiers of Kansas or Manitoba.

Another, more frantic pilgrimage began 50 years later. By the time it peaked, some 40,000 Mennonites had forever deserted the country they had called home since 1789.

It seemed that history was repeating itself. There had been many contented years of growth, but now political ferment gnawed at the Mennonite sinew. As in Polish-Prussia a hundred years earlier, Mennonites mobilized in response to external pressures. Once again, a military reality completely beyond them unleashed events that tightened the noose around the lifestyle they had sought so earnestly to protect.

The first Russian migration

Russia's loss of the Crimean War (1853-56) to Britain and France was a wake-up call to Russian nationalists. As so often happens when a country loses face, suspicion

Economic factors as well as fear of growing Russian nationalism and the perceived threat of lost religious freedom led many Mennonites to emigrate to Canada. The first immigrants to arrive in Manitoba docked here at the Forks of the Red and Assiniboine rivers in downtown Winnipeg.

and prejudice against minorities grew. Foreigners were quick to feel the chill, not only the Mennonites, but also other immigrant groups like Jews, Poles, and Germans.

A new call to arms to ensure military might was restored. There was talk of mandatory conscription. What would happen to the guaranteed Mennonite exemption from military service? Those with long memories recalled that this was how their troubles had begun in Polish-Prussia a century earlier.

A worrisome era of Russification unfolded as the country sought to cleanse itself of foreign impediments. It irked Russians that so many Mennonites who had lived their whole lives in Russia could not speak their language. Government "reforms" sought to elevate the Russian language. Official correspondence was henceforth to be in Russian, and there were efforts to have Russian taught in schools across the land. This was a major blow for the Mennonites, whose colonies were islands of German (and its cousin tongue, Low German) in a Slavic sea.

After so many years of being left alone, many Mennonites felt their special status seeping away. One of their greatest fears—assimilation—loomed.

North America beckons

Around this time, in one of the great *deja vu* moments in Mennonite history, the central plains of North America were opening up to settlement.

Like the Russia of a hundred years before, the United States needed settlers to populate the vast prairies and sustain the greatest commercial development of the century—the railroad. The Santa Fe Railroad was anxious to see homesteading in places like Kansas and Nebraska.

Canada, meanwhile, yearned to populate the prairies, until now occupied only by aboriginal people. Earlier French, British, and Scottish settlers had clustered along the river banks. But settlers were needed to go inland, where iron rails would soon slice across this new country which had just come into being in 1867.

With the prospect of free land and freedom of conscience, many Mennonites understandably lost interest in an uncertain future in Russia.

The first wave of emigration began in 1873-74, with about a third of the Russian Mennonites (18,000) leaving for North America. Some 10,000 of these, mostly from Molotschna, went to the United States (Kansas, Nebraska, Dakota, and Minnesota). The other 8,000 from the more conservative Chortitza and other colonies went to Canada (Manitoba). As in the past, their motives were mixed. Some left because they saw their cherished freedoms threatened; some were attracted by economic opportunity.

Why did 70 percent of the Mennonites choose to stay in Russia? Some were too comfortable to leave; some did not see the threat quite as keenly. One elder wrote: "Some consider it a matter of conscience to go; I consider it a matter of conscience to stay. . . . We are to be the salt of the earth, and salt is needed here as much as anywhere else" (Dyck 1967, p. 157).

Many felt inclined to be salt in some new place.

In the hindsight of history, various interpretations of this event have been put forward. One view is that those who left in the 1870s were not at the cutting edge, either culturally or economically. These perhaps hoped they could once again replicate the past.

Many of those who stayed in Russia had more to lose economically if they left. It was hard to pull up stakes when things were going well. They hoped the winds of Russification were merely zephyrs and that an even better future lay ahead. Up to a point, they were correct, for the initial threat of Russification did wane. To some, the conservatives' departure was a cleansing purge, giving the remaining "progressives" more freedom to advance. Moreover, many departing Mennonites sold their land at bargain prices, alleviating the perpetual problem of the landless and giving many others a chance to add to their holdings.

Another exodus

Fifty years later, a second great trek to North America was triggered, again by political and military upheaval. Even before the Bolshevik Revolution of 1917, Mennonites had fallen into sharp disfavor. There was plenty of opposition from the Orthodox Church, which regarded them as a sect. And then there was the fallout from World War I (1914-18) in which Germany was the enemy of Russia.

As Mennonites became more settled and prosperous, they imported design features from Europe, such as the ornate stylings on the Johan Peters residence in Neu Halbstadt, Russia.

In the eyes of the Russians, there was little to distinguish the Mennonites from Germans. Even while Germany loomed as the enemy, the Mennonites persisted in using the German language. Culturally, they had been dining at German tables for a long time. Mennonite businesspeople had significant economic ties with Germany. The best Mennonite students went to study there. Now the Mennonites would pay a price for this secondary identity. Many Russians saw them as disloyal German separatists.

The Bolsheviks found other reasons to dislike the Mennonites. For one thing, the Mennonites represented capitalist success, which the Bolsheviks despised. And they represented yet another point of contention: religious faith. "The Bolshevik revolutionaries identified the church with all the weaknesses of Russia, including the economic exploitation of the peasants," wrote Frank H. Epp (1962, p. 9).

An explosive end to the Golden Era

The Mennonites couldn't believe how suddenly their Golden Age was smothered by persecution, plunder, and starvation. For those who had stayed, the wrenching 1920s would forever define the Mennonite experience in Russia.

Many published family histories have recounted the horrific campaign of terror visited upon the Mennonites following the revolution. Ravaging bands of anarchists laid waste to many villages in both major colonies, raping and pillaging as they went. The carnage was sporadic but brutal. Hundreds of Mennonites, including infants and

Many successful Mennonites amassed large estates outside of the Mennonite colonies. This is the Jakob Goossen estate at Wintergruen, South Russia, in 1900.

Famine in Russia in the 1920s prompted North American Mennonites to respond with a relief effort that developed into Mennonite Central Committee. The former Jacob Dyck residence in Rosental, Russia, served as the first soup kitchen to dispense food.

old men, were murdered. Some were gruesomely decapitated.

In some cases, former peasants from the Mennonite estates joined the revolutionary forces and sought out landowners who had mistreated them. Conversely, some Mennonites who had been good to their peasant help were spared.

Later, thousands were sent to labor camps in Siberia and never heard from again. Many perished from starvation or cold. Families were permanently torn apart.

The Mennonites made easy targets. They lived in relative seclusion, and they were not accustomed to fighting back.

But this time they did. Some Mennonite men could not stand idly by while roaming bandits took their pleasure. A Mennonite militia was formed to protect the villages from harm. The *Selbstschutz* (literally, self-protection), as it was called, existed during the winter of 1918-19. Its numbers reached 2,700 young men who had received rudimentary training and some weapons, mostly rifles and a few machine guns, from the retreating German army. These "soldiers" fought the anarchist Nestor Makhno and his marauders on a number of occasions.

Later on, many who participated in this army repented. Not only had they been ineffective, they had compromised the Mennonite peace stance in a way that hadn't occurred since the Anabaptist peasant revolt at Muenster in 1534.

The revolution turned the Mennonites' fortunes upside down. Crop failures followed anarchy in the early 1920s. From 1919 to 1924 famine stalked the land. Despite severe food shortages, many Mennonites shared their dwin-

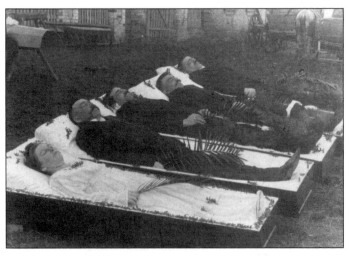

The Mennonite world exploded with the Bolshevik Revolution. Roving anarchist bands laid waste to many villages and murdered hundreds of Mennonites. In the above photo, five members of a Thiessen family, murdered in their home in January, 1918, are laid out for a funeral service.

Emigrating Mennonites hold a worship service at the train station in Lichtenau.

dling supplies with neighbors and even, in some cases, with invaders who came to do harm. The late J. B. Toews recalled his father saying, "We cannot keep food for ourselves while other people are dying." Toews said people in his village became so desperate they ate cats and dogs. "The day came when we as a family consumed our last remnant of bread baked from the flour of corn milled together with corn cobs; not very nutritious but something to fill the stomach" (1995, p. 25).

It was in response to this need that the forerunner of Mennonite Central Committee (now an international relief and development agency) came into being in 1920. Relief work began in earnest, saving countless Mennonites from an even sadder fate. To the end of the 20th century, many Mennonite families in Canada still spoke warmly of the relief work of Peter C. Hiebert, himself a descendant of earlier Russian Mennonites.

Mennonites began to leave Russia as soon as they were able. This time they went to Canada, as the United States was no longer open to receiving them. Between 1923 and 1929, 23,000 Mennonites left. Another diaspora was under way.

The third wave

A third wave of Russian emigration took place during and immediately after World War II. When the German army retreated from Russia in 1943, some 35,000 Russian Mennonites were evacuated to Poland and Western Europe. For many of them, it was a short-lived reprieve from Stalinist horrors. In the post-war negotiations, Russia and the Allied troops forced two-thirds of them to return to Russia. Most of the rest (often estimated at 12,000) went to South America (Paraguay, Uruguay, and Argentina); some went to live with relatives in Canada.

Pivotal to this mid-century exodus was the work of Mennonite Central Committee and its European representatives, C. F. Klassen, Peter J. and Elfrieda Dyck, and others. Besides working tirelessly in Europe to arrange safe passage for as many Russian Mennonites as they could, they criss-crossed North America to tell their story and enlist financial contributions from the wider Mennonite family.

The evacuation of post-war Mennonite refugees is a dramatic story of rescue and resettlement. Often lost in its telling, however, is the fate of those many thousands who were forced to return to Stalin's terror. Their stories only began to emerge in the 1970s when Mennonites started arriving in Germany as a result of Willy Brandt's *Ostpolitik*.

5.
Settlers Again

The first large-scale movement of Mennonites from Russia began in 1873 and lasted nearly a dozen years. It was an orderly migration, because the people were under no external pressure to leave. In fact, the government didn't want them to leave, and once it grasped the extent of the movement, it took steps to moderate the policies which so offended the Mennonites. But by then, many had already made up their minds.

The emigration began with a trickle in 1872, then gathered steam the following year. From 1873 to 1884, some 18,000 Mennonites left. This was about a third of all the Mennonites in Russia at the time.

Turkey Red comes to Kansas

Both Canada and the United States were greatly interested in these new settlers. More than half the immigrants, about 10,000, ended up in the United States. Several Mennonite "inspectors" from the plains states had gone to Russia to check out the possibilities of steering the newcomers to their regions. One of these was Bernhard Warkentin, who later became a wealthy miller and a leading citizen in Newton, Kansas (where his home has been turned into a museum).

The Santa Fe Railroad Company, hungry to populate the Midwest with new customers, offered cheap land from its huge reserves, as well as other inducements like freight subsidies and temporary shelter. It even chartered a steamship to transport Mennonites' goods and implements across the Atlantic.

Large groups of Russian Mennonites began settling in the central United States in 1873. Half came to Kansas; the rest put down stakes in Nebraska, Minnesota, and Dakota.

Most of those who came to Kansas during this early period ended up in the General Conference Mennonite Church, which had been established in Iowa in 1860. Smaller numbers of Mennonite Brethren and Krimmer Mennonite Brethren also came, settling in the Hillsboro and Buhler areas.

The Mennonites had hoped they would be allowed to acquire large tracts of land like those who went to Manitoba. But the United States had rules against individuals amassing so much land in a block. The Mennonites lodged an appeal, which reached the floor of the U.S. Senate but was rejected.

This made it difficult to duplicate the village pattern they had enjoyed in Russia. Nonetheless, two villages were tried, but neither enjoyed long-term success. One was settled by a Krimmer Mennonite Brethren group at Gnadenau, near Hillsboro. Another attempt was by the 600-member Alexanderwohl congregation, which emigrated from Russia virtually en masse to near Goessel. According to C. Henry Smith, all but seven families of this large congregation came together. When they left Russia, "there were no sad farewell scenes, because there was nobody to say goodbye to" (1950, p. 454).

"The Mennonites who came to Kansas in the 1870s settled at the crossing of the trails," explained historian

James Juhnke. "A few miles southwest of the spot where
the Chisholm cattle trail crossed the Santa Fe trail, Mennonite ploughs bit the sod and turned the dew under. The
prairie grasses, which had waved at passing wagon trains
and cattle herds, now yielded to the productive tyranny
of Russian Turkey red winter wheat" (1975, p. 1).

Almost immediately the people began to prosper. Their
imported wheat flourished in the rich, new soil and
brought a good price. (To this day, the hard winter wheat
of Kansas is among the best in the world.) With every
passing harvest, the Mennonite roots went deeper.

They wasted no time strengthening their spiritual bonds
through church and conference organization. Those of
General Conference affiliation helped establish Bethel College (Newton) in 1887. The Mennonite Brethren started Tabor College, 25 miles northeast, in 1908.

If the Russian Mennonites had second thoughts about
missing out on religious guarantees, they soon got over it.
Life in the new country was good.

In analyzing the Russian Mennonites' adaptation to
Kansas soil, James Juhnke raised a question that has puz-
zled historians. Why did these Mennonites, who had
adamantly resisted compromise with the governing authorities back in Russia, eagerly flock to a place that
made no promise of military exemption? Was the lure of
cheap land that tempting?

Clearly they had fallen under the spell of the Santa Fe
Railroad, which had sweet-talked them with repeated assurances that the U.S. Constitution protected individual
rights and freedom of conscience. For the naive new immigrants, these assurances apparently were enough.

"The immigration of the Mennonites was a political
act," wrote Juhnke. "It had to do with power. It had to do
with the ability of these people to keep control over their

own lives, their language, their education, their practice of nonresistance, and in fact their entire way of life . . . . They sought freedom as the power to maintain their distinctive and severely disciplined communities" (1975, p. 2).

Any such power, however, would be elusive. As Juhnke noted, they soon encountered "a challenge to their autonomy and power of self-control which was as severe as the more obvious threats of Russianization from which they fled. In Kansas they were faced with American county commissioners, American tax assessors, American school boards, and eventually American draft board officials" (p. 2).

Thus began Russian Mennonites' acculturation in the United States. Unlike in Canada, their numbers were not fed with an infusion of fresh stock in the 1920s. It was the Canadians, their ranks swollen again with thousands of German-speaking newcomers, who became a more visible manifestation of modern Russian Mennonitism that persists today.

Canada's first wave

The first Mennonites to arrive in Manitoba came by boat down the Red River to present-day Winnipeg in 1874. Some merely purchased supplies and moved on another 20 miles to where the Red and Rat rivers meet. From there they continued on by wagon to their allotted land. It was a primitive region they were entering. Previous settlers had clung to the safety of riverbanks. These immigrants were going inland, where until only a few years before the fur trade had dominated.

Initially two large tracts were set aside in Manitoba—the West and East Reserve, referring to lands on either side of the Red River. Eventually a collegial rivalry arose between the two reserves, and to this day people jest about whether someone is from *"ditsied"* (this side) or *"jantsied"* (the other side).

Once again the Mennonites recreated the village pattern they had left, even borrowing place names from the homeland. Some of these still exist, villages like Chortitz and Rosenort, as well as more thriving communities like Altona and Steinbach.

Life on the prairie revolved around church, work, and family. Routines varied little from one family to the next. As Mennonites had done everywhere else, they relied heavily on neighborly mutual aid. No one was alone when it came time to build a house or barn. The rhythms of the farm were communal. Families got together to slaughter hogs and make sausage. When someone died, neighbors got together to build a casket and to help the family prepare the body.

Family activities revolved around making the farm work and putting up its produce to last the winters, which were harsher than those the Mennonites had left behind. In winter, blocks of ice were cut from frozen ponds and stored in sheds to stay into summer. Vegetables and fruits were preserved in jars. Meats were smoked.

Church dominated spiritual life. For Mennonite young people, church meetings and choir practice were the way to meet one another. Even at weddings the church came first. A marriage ceremony was a simple event, tacked on to the end of a Sunday worship service. Sometimes, but not always, the sermon had something to do with the impending marriage.

For the first settlers, the exclusive village pattern took on mythic, almost sacred, dimensions. Exposures from the outside world were suspect.

When the Canadian Pacific Railway built a siding near Hoffnungsfeld, in the heart of Manitoba Mennonite country, the church would not permit Isaac Wiens, the Mennonite farmer on the adjacent piece of land, to use his ground for a townsite. That was thought to present an unwholesome image and would speed worldly encroachment. Besides, the town might be named after him, which would cause pride. A solution was found when the farmer agreed to swap a parcel of land with Valentine Winkler, an "English" businessman, landowner, and later politician. Thus the townsite was developed and named Winkler (instead of Wiens).

Only in a few areas did the village system last beyond the turn of the century. As new equipment came along, it became more efficient to cultivate in larger blocks. In early 1890, the newspaper in the town of Morden carried this prescient comment: "One by one the Mennonite villages established some years ago by the pioneers in Manitoba are fast disappearing. The pretty village of Hoffnungsfeld, probably the finest in this part of the country, is to be broken up this spring, the owners of the houses will move them on their farms, and it will not be many years before a Mennonite village will be a curiosity" (book manuscript by John J. Friesen, "History of Mennonites in Manitoba").

The writer was correct. Today, however, there still exist pale remnants of the old Mennonite village. Two of the best-preserved examples are Reinland and Neubergthal.

Beginning in Russia, farming was regarded as a vocation of elevated, almost sacred, status. The first Mennonite to become a merchant in the town of Winkler was nearly excommunicated. Another Mennonite who set up a general store faced ostracism from fellow Mennonites as late as 1920. In order to attract business, he introduced sales to his community. The Mennonites gradually began patronizing his store. They may have regarded him as fallen, but, after all, a bargain was a bargain.

Fear of worldliness and modernism (the two terms were often interchangeable) kept some Mennonites from progressing agriculturally. Among some, new ideas were suspect. A popular Low German comment regarding education was *Ji meha jiliehit, Ji meha fitchiehit* ("the more learned, the more misguided"). This view extended to farming practices. Those who tested new methods, like rotating crops instead of periodically leaving fields fallow for the summer, were often ridiculed.

Neighboring regions weren't far behind Manitoba in attracting Mennonites when land became scarce in the 1890s. Large numbers settled in Saskatchewan and Alberta. In time they moved farther west and east, as fruit farms and canneries offered economic opportunities in British Columbia and Ontario.

Canada's next wave

The second great movement of Mennonites to Canada was more urgent and dramatic. As mentioned in Chapter 4, the wrenching upset of the Bolshevik Revolution was a catastrophe for the Mennonites in Russia. (The classic film, *Dr. Zhivago*, though not about Mennonites, closely depicts part of their milieu.) Their departure (in many cases, escape) spanned the years 1922-30. During this period 21,000 went to Canada, and 2,600 to South America.

Modes of travel varied, depending on when during that span of time the departure took place. At first, many left in orderly fashion. Others had to be jammed into cattle cars to get them out of Russia as quickly as possible. A few, like the legendary Harbin group in 1929, fled in the dead of night in horse-drawn cutters across a frozen river to China.

The prime minister of Canada during the second major wave of Mennonite immigration was William Lyon

Mackenzie King, a Liberal from Ontario who was well acquainted with Swiss-German Mennonites in his region and held them in high regard. It was no stretch for him to feel well disposed to open the door to more Mennonites. He was exceedingly generous to the Russian newcomers, and

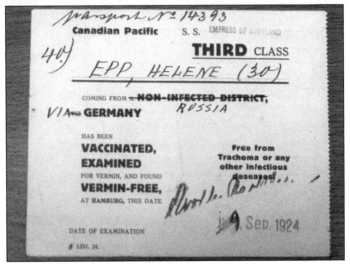

Travel documents for 1920s Russian Mennonite emigrants.

Russian passport used by a Russian Mennonite emigrant.

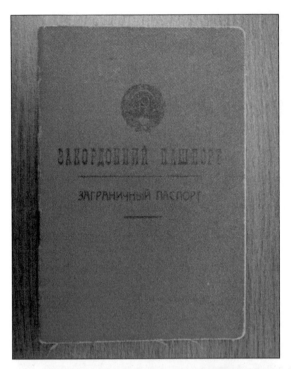

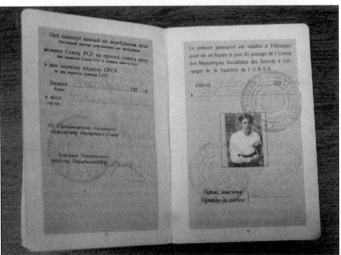

Obtaining passports became difficult in the later 1920s.

Top: People at Lichtenau train station in preparation for departure in 1924.

Bottom: Beleaguered Mennonite emigrants wait at the train in Germany, en route to South America in 1930.

Top: Departing emigrants put on a brave face as they left loved ones. Many of those who stayed behind would suffer great pain and loss.

Bottom: From 1922-1930, twenty-one thousand Mennonites left Russia for Canada; 2,600 went to South America.

Top: *For many Mennonites, this farewell would be perma-nent.*

Bottom: *People at Lichtenau train station in preparation for departure in 1924.*

Departing Mennonites heaved sighs of joy and relief when their train approached this sign of freedom, the Red Gate at the Latvian border.

they never forgot it. For the next 30 years, they faithfully voted Liberal in Canada's federal elections. Only in the late 1950s did they switch their allegiance in significant numbers to other political parties.

One of the few entry restrictions the Canadian government imposed was a ban on immigrants afflicted with trachoma, a contagious eye disease. This was a common malady in Russia, and hundreds of Mennonites had to postpone their exit or were delayed for long periods in England or Germany for treatment. Some put the delay to good use. C. A. DeFehr, a prominent businessman from Millerovo, Russia, spent his convalescence in Germany, establishing dealership contacts to sell cream separators and hardware when he arrived in Winnipeg. He became equally adept at business and conference work. An entrepreneurial statesman, he helped launch numerous Mennonite institutions and worked tirelessly to settle later Mennonite refugees in South America.

The peak year of emigration was 1924. Obtaining passports was not immediately a problem but later became one. By 1927 things tightened. Canada pulled back the welcome mat, and Russia made it harder to leave. Russia wasn't anxious to lose its best farmers, no matter how badly it had treated them. Nor was the new Communist regime happy about the image fleeing Mennonites presented to the world.

Many thousands of Mennonites were not able to leave. Their farms were confiscated. Their churches were closed and used as granaries or pool halls. Many Mennonite men were exiled to hard labor in Siberian mines.

Moving the people

The campaign to bring Mennonites to Canada following the Bolshevik Revolution turned into a monumental people-moving phenomenon.

Not all Canadian Mennonites were immediately stirred to compassion by the horrific plight of their brothers and sisters. Considerable opposition and skepticism had to be overcome.

Then, what some have described as an instinctive Mennonite skill for organization blossomed as the need arose for a church-wide structure. This institution was the Canadian Mennonite Board of Colonization, formed in 1921. Its visionary was a Saskatchewan Mennonite by the name of David B. Toews.

Toews became the liaison with the Canadian Pacific Railway (CPR), whose steamship and rail network would bring the refugees to Canada. The CPR generously advanced credit to the colonization board, and by 1924 this debt reached $800,000. (At that time, the Canadian dollar was worth a bit more than the U.S. dollar.)

Even the CPR's deep pockets weren't bottomless, and the time came when some evidence of repayment was required. The board became desperate. There were so many more people wanting to come to the Americas. Toews criss-crossed the country, pleading with Mennonite churches—both Swiss-German Mennonite and earlier Russian Mennonite immigrants—to dig deep to help reduce the debt. But their gifts were not enough.

At one critical point, the campaign was granted a reprieve by A. R. Kaufman, a German businessman who manufactured rubber boots in Ontario. Kaufman, who had already contributed heavily to the emigration cause, came up with another $25,000, a considerable sum in those days. He wrote to the CPR that his business instincts told him to hang on to the money, but he would run the risk of parting with it if it meant the difference between rescuing Mennonites or letting them freeze or starve in Russia. His generosity made it possible for an additional 9,712 Russian Mennonite emigrants to come to Canada, nearly half of all those who came.

Wrestling with debt

This act of generosity permitted the emigration to continue but did not solve the problem of the *reiseschuld* (travel debt). Many immigrants felt burdened by the amounts of their debts. The responsibility weighed heavily on the collective Mennonite consciousness, for these were people who had never been shirkers.

But repayment was not a simple matter. There were other expenses related to starting anew. Some took the attitude that the CPR could wait; right now it was more urgent to invest in farms. Poor crops aggravated the problem.

The grapevine had a way of communicating who had paid and who hadn't. Those who repaid often felt superior.

The travel debt eventually reached a total of $2 million. A massive church-wide campaign was mounted to collect it. Many people still refused to pay, and others paid in their stead. By the time David Toews died in 1947, the entire debt had been paid.

Kanadier? Or *Russlaender?*

Canada now had two different kinds of Russian Mennonites: those who had come in the 1870s, and those who arrived in the 1920s. There were significant differences between the two groups, and those differences were not easily overlooked.

The first group was more culturally and religiously conservative. At the time they left Russia, the Mennonites had not yet come into the Golden Age of high achievement in education, business, and culture. The second group, those who had stayed, had prospered economically, culturally, and intellectually.

The first group became known as *Kanadier* Mennonites (Canadians) in contrast to the more educated and urbane *Russlaender* (Russians) who came in the 1920s. (Ironically, those with the name "Canadian" found it much more difficult to fully embrace Canadian life than those who were called "Russian.")

Regardless of the feelings they may have had, the *Kanadiers* put out the welcome mat for the new immigrants. They planted extra potatoes in their gardens and raised more pigs to help feed the newcomers. They provided accommodations and jobs.

Still, the two groups found reasons not to get along. The *Russlaenders* couldn't always hide their disdain for the *Kanadiers*, whom they saw as uneducated, uncultured, hidebound, and withdrawn.

The *Kanadiers*, for their part, grew impatient with the newcomers. In general, wrote Frank H. Epp, they thought the *Russlaender* were "too proud, too aggressive, too enthusiastic about higher education, too anxious to exercise leadership, too ready to compromise with the state, too ready to move to the cities" (1982, p. 243).

The *Russlaender* "were still very much what the years of prosperity and co-operation with the tsarist state had made them. They were culturally sophisticated, for the most part better educated, progressive in their outlook, and quite aggressive in their style, all of which suggested *Hochmut* (high-mindedness or pride) or even arrogance" (Epp 1982, p. 245).

It is hard, from today's vantage point, to grasp the depth of the resentment that sometimes arose between these two groups.

One *Russlaender* woman who migrated to Manitoba in the 1920s told the story of her *Russlaender* minister, a recent widower, choosing a *Kanadier* as his second wife.

"I broke into sobs when I heard the news. I couldn't imagine that my beloved minister would do such a thing."

Such views softened over time. Hers certainly did. She later married a *Kanadier* herself.

Sharing burdens

Christian mutual aid has always been a pillar of the Anabaptist support system. Analysts have debated whether mutual aid on the prairies was an effort to survive as a separate people, or a desire to flesh out the New Testament's Sermon on the Mount, or both.

Whatever the motivation, the mutual aid instinct followed the Mennonites to the Canadian west. The settlers imported their civic and social structures from Russia. One of them, the *Waisenamt* (orphans' fund), went back all the way to Polish-Prussia. Initially a fund to manage finances for widows and orphans in the community, it became a catch-all term for a much larger mutual aid response and grew into a financial institution in its own right.

The philosophy behind the cooperative and credit union movements found ready kinship among Russian Mennonites, who soon formed their own cooperatives. Some supported cooperatives because the philosophy had the familiar ring of mutual aid; others may have seen it as a practical necessity during the difficult 1930s. Over time, the Mennonites formed a variety of insurance societies, including fire, storm, and burial.

As they had done with success in Russia, the Mennonites launched their own seniors' homes and hospitals. Concordia Hospital, for example, started by Mennonites in Winnipeg in 1930, is a modern healthcare facility today.

Various levels of education were addressed. Bethel College (Kansas) was established in 1887. Mennonite Collegiate Institute got under way in Manitoba in 1889. Tabor College (Kansas) was started by the Mennonite Brethren in 1908. Bible schools sprouted across the prairies, their schedules often set to coincide with the crop year so young people could finish their studies in time to help with spring seeding, and not resume until after fall harvest. By the beginning of World War II, Russian Mennonites in Canada had 30 Bible schools from Ontario to British Columbia.

The surge of Russian immigrants to Canada in the 1920s bolstered readership demographics for an emerging Mennonite publishing industry. Mennonite Church publisher John F. Funk began publishing for Russian Mennonites in the late 1870s with the *Nebraska Ansiedler,* which would grow into the *Mennonitische Rundschau* and function as a major inter-Mennonite weekly for Russian Mennonites. The *Rundschau* eventually became part of the Mennonite Brethren publishing program. Now more than 120 years old, it is still published, but its German audience keeps shrinking.

On the road again

Most of the Russian immigrants, especially those who came in the 1920s, were in Canada to stay. But significant groups of earlier immigrants (often called Old Colony Mennonites) grew restless. They chafed under the press of modernity in general, but the spark that set the fire was emerging government restrictions regarding education.

In the 1920s, 6,000-7,000 Old Colony Mennonites left Manitoba and Saskatchewan because the government wanted more of a hand in teaching their children. This was seen as a threat to the Old Colony way, and thousands began moving en masse to Mexico. At the time they had money, enough eventually to buy a third of a million acres of land. Mexico let them run their own village schools and do as they pleased to maintain spiritual, intellectual, and technological isolation. They clung to old ways as a tenet of faith, shunning improvements like rubber tires on tractors. In later years, others migrated for similar reasons to Belize and Bolivia.

In 1927, some of the same forces led other disgruntled Canadian Mennonites to Paraguay, where they formed Menno Colony, one of three large colonies in Paraguay's Chaco. Three years later they were joined by yet another group of refugees from Russia who wanted to go to Canada but found the doors now closed. Paraguay welcomed these people—with background political themes that sounded familiar: Paraguay wanted these settlers to bolster its claim to the Chaco and thus serve as a buffer against neighboring Bolivia which also claimed ownership. A third wave of immigration began in 1947, composed largely of refugees from World War II.

The boundaries between the Mennonites of Canada and those in Central and South Americas have remained permeable. Increasing numbers of Mennonites from Belize and Mexico, nudged by dwindling economic prospects at home and, in some cases, by a desire for a more ventilated way of life, have drifted back to Canada. A few have found new homes in places like Nova Scotia. Larger numbers have settled in places near Leamington, Ontario, and Taber, Alberta.

6.
The Rural-Urban Shift

The Mennonites in the Golden Age in Russia may have shaken off their village, separatist mentality. But geographically, they remained mostly rural, as they did in North America until the 1930s. Then many began to leave their cherished farms for the urban world.

Along with the Okies depicted so poignantly in John Steinbeck's *The Grapes of Wrath*, Mennonites from Oklahoma and Kansas clambered out of the dust bowl of the Great Depression and headed west for the fruit basket of California. They settled near places like Fresno, Bakersfield, and later San Jose.

An architectural feature brought to the Canadian prairies by Russian Mennonites was to connect the house and barn. This house/barn is still in use in southern Manitoba.

In Canada the physical distance from village to city was short, usually less than a hundred miles. But the cultural distance was great.

Farming was the dominant occupation of Mennonites in Russia, as it was for those who migrated to Canada and the United States in the 1870s. This was less so for those

A Mennonite-owned general store in Winkler, Manitoba, around 1915. Being in business was controversial for Mennonites at the time.

who came in the 1920s. New occupational pursuits had opened with the expanding Golden Age in Russia. Many went into the teaching profession or business. But those who arrived in Canada in the 1920s were expected by those who welcomed them to be farmers. Many who were ill-suited to the task were among the first to leave the land when they got the chance.

Along urban trails

One avenue to an expanded urban consciousness was Christian outreach. As early as 1915 the Krimmer Mennonite Brethren, who had settled in rural South Dakota, opened a mission church in Chicago. They also worked among African Americans in North Carolina, and today a small conference of half a dozen congregations is active there.

In Winnipeg, German-speaking Mennonite churches began to emerge in the first decade of the 20th century to meet the spiritual needs of recent arrivals, including other groups like Lutherans. For the Russian Mennonites, German was the language of worship and congregational discourse for many years. The eventual cultural clash over language was complex and lengthy, as German became the lightning rod for a host of struggles surrounding urbanization.

German was an issue in Canada for much longer than in the United States. The Russian Mennonites who settled in the U.S. Midwest may have wanted to preserve German as their preferred language, but they were discouraged from doing so by harsh anti-German sentiments following World War I (including the burning of a church in Kansas). Unlike Canada, the United States did not receive a fresh infusion of immigrants in the 1920s to nourish the

German profile. Among the Russian Mennonites of Canada, however, friction over the erosion of German and the increase of English persisted for many years. By the beginning of the 1960s, a number of churches in Canada still used both German and English in their services. But this dwindled to a handful by the end of the century.

Mennonite "maids"

A leading edge of emerging urbanization were the "Mennonite domestics," a unique chapter in the story of Russian Mennonites in Canada.

Many single female immigrants, as well as young women from the farms, began to find jobs as live-in domestic helpers in the homes of affluent city-dwellers. They typically received lodging and a monthly stipend, which many sent home to bolster family finances.

These young transplants faced an utterly new urban environment where language, culture, and lifestyle were all different from their upbringing. To help them cope, Mennonite "girls homes" came into being. In Winnipeg, for instance, both the Mennonite Brethren (1925) and the General Conference (1926) operated girls homes. These were large private residences, run by Mennonite matrons, which served as a homey refuge for the women on Sundays and days off. They were islands of fellowship in an urban sea. The mandate of the matrons grew to include employment referrals, advocacy, and even mediation with difficult employers.

Both Winnipeg homes served more than a thousand women each until finally closing in 1959. Similar homes operated in Saskatoon, Saskatchewan; Calgary, Alberta; and Vancouver, British Columbia.

Some alumni looked back on this experience as participating in a "Mennonite finishing school." This is where

*A Mennonite Brethren immersion baptism service in south-
ern Manitoba during the 1930s. For many years mode of baptism was a thorny issue among some Russian Mennonite immigrants to Canada and the United States.*

they learned "city manners" and sampled upscale living.
They developed a taste for new foods like scones and
marmalade. They learned how to prepare roast beef and
Yorkshire pudding and how to set a refined table. When
they returned to their farm families or started their own
households, they brought along their new exposures and
perhaps an emerging fondness for finery. Some analysts
have blamed this phase of pioneer history with sowing
the seeds of materialism. At the very least, it sped the
process of urbanization.

After the farm

What did people do after they left the farm? A natural
segue for many was into farm-related businesses. Black-
smiths, for example, found new commercial prospects in
metal fabrication and machine work, leading to the manufacture of trailers and truck bodies. The economic boom
after World War II offered plenty of room to people who
were handy with tools. Mennonites became successful
carpenters, masonry contractors, and homebuilders.

Construction components and hardware were other logical extensions of these people's skills. They developed large companies to manufacture trusses, windows, and kitchen cabinets. Some went into furniture-making, such as A. A. DeFehr, formerly of Millerovo, Russia. In the mid-1940s he began making wooden step stools in his Winnipeg basement. Today the DeFehr company, known as Palliser Furniture, is the largest casegoods manufacturer in Canada and the largest private employer in the province of Manitoba.

As Mennonites became increasingly fluent in the vocabulary of the city, they branched beyond their traditional agricultural base. They distinguished themselves in businesses ranging from bus lines and trucking to printing and broadcasting. Their entrepreneurial skills were fortified by a growing Mennonite labor force of loyal employees with a strong work ethic.

Guided by a cooperative spirit, Mennonite immigrants set up their own financial institutions. Some, like this modern credit union in Rosenort, Manitoba, have become highly successful.

Wherever there is agriculture, Mennonites will thrive. Here a Russian Mennonite descendant enjoys oranges, one of several crops grown widely by Mennonites in California's central valley.

Putting down institutional roots

Russian Mennonites have traditionally looked after their own. Wherever they went they set up institutions to care for the unfortunate. In Russia this included hospitals, eldercare facilities, orphanages, even a school for the deaf. In North America, the move to the city included the formation of institutions to assist the needy and to nurture faith and community. Hospitals were started in various cities, among them today's thriving Concordia Hospital in Winnipeg. Like Mennonites elsewhere in North America, the Russian Mennonites set up credit unions and insurance companies. Steinbach Credit Union (Manitoba) and Niagara Credit Union (Ontario) are among Canada's 10 largest credit unions today. Summer camps began to make their appearance in the late 1940s. Religious publishing ventures were born.

For the Russian Mennonites, the 1940s were a time of new urban initiatives in education. Earlier Mennonite colleges had been located in towns rather than in large cities. In 1944 American Mennonite Brethren established Pacific Bible Institute in Fresno, California. It grew into Pacific College, then Fresno Pacific College, and now Fresno Pacific University.

Mennonite Brethren Bible College, later known as Concord College and now part of Canadian Mennonite University (CMU), was launched in Winnipeg in 1944, the first college-level Mennonite school in Canada. Canadian Mennonite Bible College (now also part of CMU) came into being in 1947. Two Mennonite high schools also were formed in Winnipeg during this time.

Urban comfort level

Today the Russian Mennonites are comfortably situated in the city, although some analysts say they often retain their village attitudes. They go to church in Minneapolis, Wichita, Denver, Phoenix, Fresno, San Jose, Vancouver, Edmonton, Calgary, Saskatoon, Winnipeg, Kitchener/Waterloo, St. Catharines, and Toronto. Winnipeg, a city of 675,000, is the largest urban Mennonite community in the world. It is home to 20,000 Mennonites of Russian descent, as well as countless social institutions and an estimated 1,000 Mennonite-owned businesses.

Russian Mennonite farmers still dot the Canadian prairies and American Midwest, but their numbers have dwindled along with the larger farm population. In the three decades following World War II, the number of farmers of Russian Mennonite lineage dropped by half. Less and less are the Russian Mennonites a people of the land.

Those who still farm have become increasingly sophisticated. They are rural only in geography. They use the most up-to-date implements, rely on spreadsheets to track hog performance, and employ satellite technology to gauge fertilizer use. They drive to the city to attend concerts, church meetings, and sporting events. Even if they make their living on a farm, these people behave in many ways like urbanites.

7.
A Coat of Many Colors

Mennonites are sometimes called "a people apart." Despite their many commonalities, they seem to have little difficulty finding reasons to part company among themselves. Some historians have used the term "Mennonite sickness" to describe this schismatic tendency. Interestingly, Mennonites rarely split over doctrine but rather over how to apply the Christian faith they hold in common. This is true of Mennonites around the world, and the Russian Mennonites are no exception.

When the Mennonites left Russia they were a variety of groups, like a rope of intertwined cords. Some of these cords would unravel into fraying strands. Keeping track of them isn't easy.

The churches formed in Russia

The largest numbers of Russian Mennonites who came to North America joined either the General Conference Mennonite Church (GCMC) or the Mennonite Brethren Church (MBC).

A point of frequent confusion has been the relationship of the Russian "Church Mennonites" (often called

Kirchliche) and the General Conference Mennonite Church. They are often spoken of as being one and the same, which may be true in spirit but is not precisely correct. The GCMC never existed by that name in Russia, having been formed in Iowa in 1860. However, immigrating Church Mennonites typically joined the GCMC when they arrived on North American soil. By the time of its centennial in 1960, the General Conference Mennonite Church membership was roughly two-thirds Russian Mennonite in background. The GCMC became part of the newly merged Mennonite Church in 2002.

A longstanding difference between various groups of Russian Mennonites has been mode of baptism. The mother church in Russia baptized by sprinkling or pouring water on the head of the candidate. When the breakaway Mennonite Brethren held their first baptism in 1860, they adopted the immersion mode (immersing one

Russian Mennonites today come in numerous flavors. Some prefer modest meetingplaces; others, like this southern Manitoba Mennonite Brethren church, are comfortable with a more modern appearance.

time backwards), which they learned from Baptist influences. They liked the symbolism of being buried with Christ and then resurrected. In the Krimmer Mennonite Brethren Church, the candidate knelt and was immersed forward.

The Mennonite Brethren have held fast to their preferred mode of baptism. Today a typical MB congregation has a baptismal font at the front, although it may be covered by panels or curtains when not in use. (In earlier times, baptisms were held outdoors in lakes or rivers.) For a hundred years the Mennonite Brethren did not accept members who had been sprinkled, unless they were rebaptized by immersion. In the 1960s the MB Conference relaxed this rule and gave individual congregations the freedom to choose whether or not to insist on immersion baptism for transfers. Today most MB churches accept sprinkled members who want to transfer in; however, they themselves practice only immersion.

The Mennonite Brethren, who owed their origins to pietist influences, continued to borrow freely from other evangelical traditions. In the early part of the 20th century, they were affected considerably by the fundamentalist stream. They tended also to ally themselves with dispensationalism and end-times theologies, although these never became part of their official doctrine and are no longer as prominent.

How else are the Mennonite Brethren and the historical General Conference groups different today? Many Mennonite Brethren are unabashed about seeing themselves as evangelicals. Those who made up the former General Conference are generally less comfortable with the public profile of evangelicalism. Some GC members might say they include evangelism as one component of the wider ministry of Christian discipleship, while MBs

Nick Rempel, longtime pastor of the Mennonite Brethren Church in Buhler, Kansas, stands before the remains of the Rueckenau MB Church, Molotschna Colony. The church, now a granary, produced Elder Abram Schellenberg, who migrated to Kansas in 1879 and became a pivotal figure in the emergence of the North American MB conference. He was a leader in the mother church of Rempel's congregation.

might be inclined to elevate evangelism to a higher plane. Some GCs think MBs talk too much of evangelism, while some MBs think GCs are too preoccupied with peace and social issues. MBs have been slower than GCs to open the door to women in ministry.

General Conference Mennonites have been somewhat more ecumenical when it comes to associating actively with other Mennonites and mainline denominations. The Mennonite Brethren can be ecumenically involved with other evangelical groups, like the Christian and Missionary Alliance and the Evangelical Free Church. But they often stand on the sidelines during inter-Mennonite discussions. Nonetheless, there is growing cooperation. The two groups jointly operate Columbia Bible College in British Columbia and have recently joined together in the formation of Canadian Mennonite University in Winnipeg. A few congregations in Canada and the United States have held joint membership in the two denominations.

Evangelical Mennonite Conference

As noted earlier, this was the first group to split from the mother church in Russia in the early 1800s. It was derisively called the *Kleine Gemeinde* (small church) at first, but eventually the name took on a more positive flavor and was claimed proudly. Today the group uses the name Evangelical Mennonite Conference (EMC).

This relatively small but energetic conference seeks to blend Anabaptism with an unapologetic evangelicalism and perhaps a dash of separatism. The EMCs have been

Like other Mennonite groups, the Russian Mennonites wanted educational institutions they could call their own. Tabor College was established by the Mennonite Brethren in Hillsboro, Kansas, in 1908.

more uneasy with the trappings of denominationalism than the General Conference and Mennonite Brethren. The conference lacks some institutional manifestations like colleges and seminaries. But it participates in the Steinbach Bible College, publishes its own periodical, and is willing to work with other groups in missions when it lacks the critical mass to carry out such efforts itself.

Two groups that date back to Russia but which no longer exist are the Krimmer Mennonite Brethren (KMB) and the *Allianz Gemeinde* (Alliance Church).

The Krimmer Mennonite Brethren Church emerged in the Crimean region of present-day Ukraine in 1869 and emigrated to the United States as a body in 1874, with many of its members settling in South Dakota and Kansas. For many years the group provided a church home for people coming out of the Hutterite tradition. The KMBs merged with the Mennonite Brethren in 1960.

The *Allianz Gemeinde* was formed in Russia in 1905 as an attempt to bridge some of the troubled baptismal waters that had been stirred up between different groups. They were known chiefly for permitting various modes of baptism—immersion, pouring, or sprinkling (hence the cooperative name *Allianz* or alliance). This group ceased to exist in North America when its members migrated to Canada, most of them joining Mennonite Brethren congregations.

Churches formed in North America

As noted earlier, splits seldom occurred because of basic doctrinal differences. A comparison of confessions of faith from various Mennonite groups shows a remarkably solid core of common beliefs, not only among Russian Mennonites, but also with Swiss-German Mennonite groups. The splits often were the product of differences in leadership, emphasis, spiritual fervor, perceptions of worldliness, or the influence of visiting evangelists.

Evangelical Mennonite Brethren

This group was formed in 1889 by Russian Mennonites in Minnesota and Nebraska who sought a more rigorous spiritual discipline than they found in existing churches. They adopted the name Evangelical Mennonite Brethren in 1937 after having first been called the Conference of United Mennonite Brethren of North America, and later the Defenseless Mennonite Brethren in Christ of North America. In the 1980s they abandoned the Mennonite name entirely, renaming themselves the Fellowship of Evangelical Bible Churches.

In 1955 the United States Mennonite Brethren opened a seminary in Fresno, California. In 1975 it became a joint seminary with the Canadian Mennonite Brethren Conference.

The list of smaller conferences can be truly perplexing, partly because some have gone through name changes but people persist in referring to them by their old names (often connected to their birthplaces in Russia). These smaller groups exist chiefly in Canada, with some in Latin America.

The Bergthaler church no longer exists as a conference but the name is still used unofficially. It was named after a daughter colony of the original Chortitza Colony. Except for a small group that still functions separately in Saskatchewan, the Bergthalers joined the Conference of Mennonites in Canada (General Conference).

The Sommerfelder church was formed in Manitoba's west reserve when a group broke away from the Bergthalers. Another group then broke away from the Sommerfelders to produce the Rudnerweider Mennonite Church, which today goes by the name of Evangelical Mennonite Mission Conference. To confuse things further, the same folks who were Sommerfelders, but who lived in the east reserve, go by the name Chortitzer Mennonites. The Old Colony Mennonites, meanwhile, are also known as Reinlander Mennonites.

While having a less visible denominational presence, these groups are not lacking in energy or vitality. Despite differences from their past, they work together cooperatively through Mennonite Central Committee.

8.
What Does A Russian Mennonite Look Like?

Can you spot a Russian Mennonite in a crowd? Not likely. Most of them blend quite readily into North American society. But there are some differences between Russian and other kinds of Mennonites, though you may need a keen eye to notice them.

First, a look at the church. When it comes to doctrine, there is little difference between Russian Mennonites and the others. Theologians who have examined the various confessions of faith see a high degree of similarity. Where the difference usually comes in is in emphasis. One group may place greater importance upon or interpret a certain doctrinal tenet differently than another.

One example might be the area of conformity to surrounding culture. Russian Mennonite groups who migrated to Central and South Americas during the 1920s have tried to resist being swept up by cultural influence from their neighbors. Other groups are more at ease about taking part in the wider culture. In North America, a Russian Mennonite is unlikely to talk about "nonconformity" while Swiss-German Mennonites, at least the older ones, often retain this word in their vocabulary.

Differences extend to the area of nonresistance. Here, Russian Mennonites (both former General Conference and Mennonite Brethren) have practiced less fully the traditional Anabaptist views. In World War II the proportion of Russian Mennonites who served in the military was noticeably higher than those from the Swiss-German Mennonite groups.

There are, of course, detectably different views on evangelism. The Mennonite Brethren Church in Manitoba got its start when MB evangelists from Minnesota ventured northward and made converts of Old Colony Mennonites. Among Old Colony Mennonites, by contrast, salvation is a quieter matter and tends to be seen as a corporate rather than individual issue. They tend to regard popular forms of evangelism as making a prideful display of spirituality.

"Do you know Low German?"

Spend any amount of time with people of Russian Mennonite background, and one will eventually hear a reference to Low German. This was the language spoken during the week in Mennonite homes in Russia. It is often considered less refined than High German, the language of worship and culture.

Actually, Low German has a distinguished background; its historic Saxon connection predates both modern German and English. University students have sometimes been amused to find that knowledge of Low German makes it easier to understand Old English literature, such as Chaucer's tales.

But the actual use of the language was less lofty. Low German is known for its colorful phrases which often cannot be accurately translated into English. In many Mennonite homes, earthy references were more readily tolerated in Low German than in either High German or English. One will still hear Low German spoken at MCC sales in Hutchinson, Kansas, and Morris, Manitoba. But fewer and fewer North Americans speak it. It is still widely used among Mennonites in Mexico and South America.

Foods that Grandma made

The traditional foods of the Russian Mennonites serve up different flavors than the apple-butter and shoofly pie of their Swiss-German Mennonite brothers and sisters. Among Russian Mennonites, a traditional meal might include *borscht* (a cabbage-based vegetable soup) and *zwieback* (double-decker buns). Another popular entree is *verenika* (dumplings filled with a cottage-cheese mixture, often served with a gravy of ham fat, onions, and cream). On a hot summer day, a Russian Mennonite family might enjoy watermelon and *rollkuchen* (flat strips of deep-fried dough—a bland taste but very addictive once acquired). For dessert many would enjoy *pluma moos,* a cold "fruit soup" made of plums or cherries. Restaurants in southern Manitoba often serve these dishes and describe them as "Mennonite food," much to the chagrin of those who understand Mennonitism as a faith rather than an ethnic culture.

"So you're not really one of us"

In Russia Mennonites became both a religious and a culturally distinctive group. Efforts to extend some of this in Canada were unsuccessful. But a legacy is that Mennonitism became identified as an ethnic peoplehood. To-day, it is common in southern Manitoba (and even in parts of the United States) for someone to be identified as a Mennonite even if that person joins a Baptist church or, conversely, abandons faith entirely.

This can lead to a form of exclusion. A man with an Irish surname who had been a member of a California Mennonite congregation for two decades was told at a church conference, "So you're not really one of us."

How do they dress?

Appearance-wise, most Russian Mennonites are indistin-guishable from anyone else on the street. Half a century ago they likely dressed more modestly than most people, and their womenfolk were slower to wear cosmetics, but those days are largely gone. In matters of dress, most Russ-ian Mennonites have assimilated completely.

Exceptions are the Church of God in Christ Mennonite (Holdeman), whose women wear prayer caps. In Central and South Americas, as well as in some areas of Manito-ba, Ontario, and Alberta, pockets of Old Colony Men-nonites also stand out. The men do not wear ties with their dark suits, and the women often wear a kerchief-type head covering and distinctive print skirts.

Participants in public life

Anabaptism has often been marked by a countercul-tural stance toward society. The Russian Mennonites' his-tory of isolated colonies was certainly countercultural to a degree. But something happened to that mentality dur-ing their Golden Age in Russia. They became more deeply immersed in the world around them and grew

Jake Epp (left) was perhaps the most successful Russian Mennonite to enter politics. He served as a Member of Parliament in Canada for more than 20 years, holding three different cabinet posts. Here he is shown visiting with residents of the village of Elisabethtal, in present-day Ukraine, from where his father emigrated in the 1920s.

comfortable in new circles of influence. This tendency accompanied them to North America where it flowered. Though the 1870s immigrants now living in Mexico, Belize, and Bolivia have staunchly resisted acculturation, large numbers of the others are more relaxed about embracing the world around them.

Russian Mennonites have more readily participated in public life than their Swiss-German counterparts. They have been quicker to take up legal and political professions. For more than 40 years Russian Mennonites have been seeking (and winning) political offices on city councils, provincial/state legislatures, and even in Parliament.

This openness to the political structures of society is noticeable when various strands of Mennonites work together on committees and in associations. Russian Mennonites often seem less resistant to political activity and tend to see larger civil society more as "us" rather than "them."

A matter of temperament

Perhaps there is still something in the Russian Mennonite genes that makes them more aggressive than their Swiss-German sisters and brothers around the conference table. The mantle of being "the quiet in the land" does not rest as comfortably on their shoulders. While Swiss-German Mennonites seem to be more reticent, reserved, and committed to process, those of Russian background seem more direct, forthright, and openly competitive. If a Swiss-German and Russian Mennonite come to differences while negotiating, it will be the Swiss-German who will suggest taking the issue back to committee. If someone is going to pound the table, it will be the Russian Mennonite.

9.
Where Are They Today?

Russian Mennonites have moved a long way from home. Their diaspora reaches from the United States and Canada into Mexico, Belize, Paraguay, and Bolivia. The ventilating winds of Gorbachev's *glasnost* enabled one

A store in the town of Cuauhtemoc, Mexico, promotes cheese, the almost exclusive domain of Mennonite producers in the area.

last out-migration from Russia to Germany, where some 100,000 immigrants of Mennonite background live today. Professionally, Russian Mennonites have come far, infiltrating business, education, social services, healthcare, medical research, agriculture, the arts, even politics. They can even be found on the sports pages and television screens of modern America.

For the most part, the Mennonites from Russia have quit their nomadic ways. The largest segments are by now thoroughly acculturated in the United States and Canada.

Even those who moved to Germany in the latter part of the 20th century seem to have settled in with relative comfort; likewise those in Paraguay, Brazil, and other parts of South America.

Some Old Colony Mennonites in Mexico, Belize, Paraguay, and Bolivia (totaling perhaps 110,000) are still restless and continue to trickle north.

A very small number remain in Ukraine and elsewhere in the former Soviet Union.

Here is a look at some of the larger pockets of Russian Mennonites.

Mennonites in Mexico

"If the Mennonites had their own Third World country, it would be the colonies of Mexico," says one longtime observer.

This is not obvious when you travel Highway 45, the paved four-lane that runs through one of the main colonies from the town of Rubio south to the city of Cuauhtemoc, about 200 miles below El Paso, Texas. Studding "the strip," as the road is called, are the businesses that form the brick and steel of economic life: grocery and produce stores, fur-

Abram Olfert, one of the more successful businesspeople in the Mexican Mennonite colonies, was excommunicated from his church many years ago for owning a vehicle. Now the majority of the Mennonites have parked their horse-drawn buggies in favor of pick-ups.

niture and appliance outlets, restaurants, implement companies, and fertilizer plants. Only a few years ago these enterprises were tucked away in villages; now their owners have ventured onto the highway.

Bright signs, neat yards, and clean restaurants present a picture of well-being. But off the highway one hears stories of desperate poverty in outlying villages.

The story of the Mexican Mennonites could be called a story about education, with issues of faith, economics, and culture twined around it like strands of rope.

Among many of the bishops who wield control, education remains in low regard. Children are schooled for a mere six or seven years, and even then are taught little more than the alphabet, the Bible, numbers, and some singing. Most teachers are untrained, sometimes knowing little more than the pupils they are teaching. Up to half of the adults may be functionally illiterate.

Illiterate people cannot read the Bible for themselves. Church services are conducted in High German, which many of the Low German-speaking colonists barely understand.

People who are unable to read do not get good jobs. Even in Mennonite-owned businesses, Mennonite workers sweep floors or stock shelves while native Mexicans work in the office. The Mennonites do not have enough education to type a letter or write out a receipt. The new credit union in Cuauhtemoc, of which the locals are very proud, has a few Mennonite managers, but most of the staff are Mexicans.

For those who leave the old church for some of the more contemporary Mennonite congregations, life holds brighter prospects. These members on the move are at the forefront

The Mennonites of Mexico are a study in contrasts. On the main highway one sees prosperous businesses, like this cooperatively-owned corn storage and fertilizer plant; off the highway are villages in desperate poverty.

of trying to modernize their fellow Mexican Mennonites. In recent years important institutions have been established, like a seniors home. A local radio station carries Low German broadcasts that educate and nurture.

The Mexican Mennonites began their move to Mexico in the 1920s when they felt they were losing control of their schools in central Canada. Later on, groups of them moved to Belize and Bolivia.

Today there is a considerable amount of movement of these Mennonites back to Canada, where they are called *Kanadier* Mennonites. Many of them take advantage of their continuing eligibility for Canadian citizenship by moving to Alberta and Ontario, often for seasonal agricultural work. There are an estimated 25,000-30,000 *Kanadier* Mennonites in Canada. Because of their distrust of the educational system, their young people leave school as early as the eighth grade.

The colonies of Paraguay

Like the Mexican Mennonites, the first Mennonites to arrive in Paraguay in 1927 left Canada over the schools issue. Three years later they were joined by refugees from Russia for whom the door to Canada had closed. The third group of immigrants to Paraguay were World War II refugees who started coming in 1947.

Most of them live in the Chaco, a dry, scrubby bushland that they have transformed into a garden.

Some 12,000 Mennonites live in the colonies established by these three groups. Another 15,000 Mennonites live in numerous smaller colonies. Some have relocated to Asuncion, the capital.

Cattle and dairy products dominate the Mennonite agricultural output, although there are also lush farms of

Fifty years ago the cows in Paraguay's Chaco produced only a few liters of milk a day. Today the Mennonite colonies furnish 60 percent of the dairy products consumed in Paraguay. Products from the Mennonite-owned Trebol dairy can be found everywhere.

corn, peanuts, castor beans, cotton, soybeans, and sesame seed. The Mennonite colonies now furnish 60 percent of the country's dairy products. The clover-shaped logo of the Trebol dairy (located in Loma Plata, the capital of Menno Colony) can be seen all over Paraguay. The leading hotels in Asuncion serve yogurt and chocolate milk from Trebol.

Mennonites also produce 30 percent of Paraguay's peanuts and 11 percent of its meat. Trucks make thousands of trips a year on the Trans-Chaco Highway (built with the help of Mennonite PAX workers in the 1950s) to transport 200,000 tons of produce from the Mennonite colonies to Asuncion.

The Mennonites are relatively well off. The per capita income of the colonies is said to be $10,000 U.S.; in the rest of the country it is $1,600.

The Mennonites here have learned to work together. One joint project is the Chaco radio station ZP-30, which

Top: Russian Mennonites began settling in Paraguay in 1927. Here, the co-op store, a beehive of commercial activity, anchors the main intersection of the town of Filadelfia.

Bottom: In 1975 Mennonites from various groups in Paraguay, supported by other Mennonites in Canada, opened ZP-30, a Mennonite-run radio station that broadcasts Christian outreach and educational programs in several indigenous languages.

since 1975 has provided news, Christian nurture, and educational programs in several indigenous languages. In the city of Asuncion, Mennonites and Mennonite Brethren worship together in a joint congregation but operate separate seminaries. Mennonite businesspeople in Asuncion run thriving companies (one manufactures up to 80 motorcycles a day) and maintain a joint chaplaincy program to benefit employees and help bolster ethical sensitivity.

A fragment in Ukraine

"Marx and Lenin must be turning in their graves. Here we are talking about two things they both despised—Christianity and business—and there they are watching it all."

It was 1990. The speaker gestured to the front wall of the large assembly hall in Kiev, Ukraine. Two massive portraits of Communist icons, Karl Marx and Vladimir Lenin, hung on the front wall, peering sternly down at the proceedings of a Christian business conference, the first to be held in the former Soviet Union in at least 70 years.

The conference had been requested the previous year by Mennonite church leaders in the Soviet Union who were enjoying the first warm breezes of *glasnost*. "Come help us," they had implored Mennonites from North America. "For 70 years we have been told that business is evil. Now we are permitted to go into business. Come tell us how we can do this without losing our souls."

The three-day conference, organized by Mennonite Economic Development Associates (MEDA) and Logos, a West German ministry, sought to explore how faith and business could work together in the post-Soviet era. Some 165 Bap-

When the Soviet Union began opening up to western enterprise, Russian Mennonite descendants worked through Mennonite Economic Development Associates (MEDA) to help Russians—both Mennonite and non-Mennonite—to learn new skills and emerge from their restrictive past. At left, a Canadian participant in the 1993 automotive seminar. At right, a local Russian guide.

tists, Pentecostals, and Mennonites attended. But the Mennonites—those who had asked for the convention—were there in small numbers. Most were at home "sitting on their suitcases" (waiting to emigrate). Their German background made it possible to emigrate to the welcoming arms of Germany, and many were taking the opportunity.

The conference led to the formation of a Moscow-based organization called the Association of Christians in Business. It continues to function as a nurturing agency today for evangelicals.

What is left of the Mennonites in the former Soviet Union? Many of the formerly large congregations have dried up. The MB church in Karaganda, for instance, once had more than a thousand members. Today it has a hundred.

Efforts have been made to stir the embers. In 1994 a new congregation was formed in the city of Zaporozhye, Ukraine, which encompasses the original Mennonite settlement of Chortitza. Mennonites were largely expelled from the area in the 1940s, but some have resurfaced or returned.

The congregation, called the Evangelical Mennonite Church of Zaporozhye, has received considerable help from North American Mennonites and from local Baptists who feel close to the Mennonites. The church is currently led by a pastor couple from Canada.

Life in the Ukraine is not easy, and the Mennonites suffer with their neighbors from a collapsed economy, erratic wages, unemployment, and moral and legal disarray. While there are regular baptisms, gains are hard to maintain because some members find the draw to Germany too hard to resist. In 2002, the membership reached 70.

The congregation has two sister churches in Ukraine: one in the former Mennonite village of Petershagen (now

Kutuzovka), and one in Mis, near Kherson. A Mennonite center has been opened in Molochansk, in the former Halbstadt girls high school. Questions have been raised as to whether there is enough Mennonite spirit to plant other churches and perhaps form a Mennonite network.

In the Omsk area there is a conference of 1,700 members in 70 small groups. This group calls itself the Union of Evangelical Christians Baptists but is composed of people of Mennonite Brethren background.

Germans open their arms

Since 1972 there has been a steady flow of remaining Mennonites from Russia to Germany. The German government provided easy entry and generous resettlement provisions to Mennonites, whom they still regarded as ethnic Germans. Today there are an estimated 100,000 immigrants of Mennonite background. There are some 350 churches in at least 10 different groups in Germany. It is not always clear whether these people are really Mennonites or want to be known as such. Back in Russia, many of those who remained during the Communist era either went underground or joined registered Baptist churches.

Theologically, these people are very conservative, shaped by their suffering under Stalin and with virtually no fresh breezes of rejuvenation coming their way. Many in North America see them as overly legalistic and too inclined to separate over what North Americans consider small matters. At the same time, the immigrants possess tremendous energy, a strong commitment to mission, and a great concern for their homeland.

Some have since migrated to join relatives in Canada, but many have made Germany their permanent home.

At home in North America

The dominant group of Russian Mennonites has never strayed beyond North America, at least not geographically. Culturally and missiologically, they span the globe. A mission-minded people, they have expanded greatly and helped establish large sister churches in India and Africa. In the United States and Canada, their outreach has touched myriad cultures. On a typical Sunday morning you

While best known for furniture manufacturing, entrepreneur Frank DeFehr is also involved in the production of flour in Manitoba. His father emigrated from the Russian town of Millerovo where the DeFehr family had a flour mill that still operates today under different ownership.

can find, in cities across North America, churches sponsored by Russian Mennonite groups worshiping in Spanish, Portuguese, Vietnamese, French, Hindi, Hmong, Laotian, Korean, Arabic, Farsi, Russian, Cantonese, and Mandarin. They have a long tradition of activity in service organizations. In the very earliest days of Mennonite Central Committee (MCC), key leaders were P. C. Hiebert, then C. F. Klassen, and Peter J. and Elfrieda Dyck. Through the years, the leaders of MCC and MCC Canada have frequently been Russian Mennonites.

C. A. DeFehr and Henry Martens were among the original founders of Mennonite Economic Development Associates (MEDA). The Canadian Foodgrains Bank was set up largely through the vision of Arthur DeFehr and for many years was headed by C. Wilbert Loewen and then Al Doerksen.

In addition to their own denominational agencies, you can find Russian Mennonites serving in World Vision, Prison Fellowship, Campus Crusade, National Religious Broadcasters, Evangelical Fellowship of Canada, and Habitat for Humanity, and in major seminaries like Fuller Theological Seminary and Trinity Evangelical Divinity School.

Making music

It has been said (by others) that in a cultural center like Winnipeg, "you need the Mennonites if you want to pull off a big musical event." Indeed, Mennonites from Russia are known worldwide for their music. The roots of the phenomenon go deep.

According to historian T. D. Regehr, "Mennonite choral singing became so popular in part because choirs became social institutions in Mennonite communities. Members were usually young people for whom village life in Russia, or everyday life on isolated Canadian farms, provided limited stimulation. Choir practices and public performances, some of which involved travel, opened new artistic vistas and allowed young people to mingle and get to know one another while engaged in activities intended to glorify God" (1996, p. 275).

Music, especially choral singing, blossomed from the 1940s onward, stimulated by the efforts of colleges. The Russian Mennonite "choral hall of fame" will surely include names like Ben Horch (an early Lutheran import), Herbert Richert, Dietrich Friesen, Jonah Kliewer, Paul Wohlgemuth, Helen Litz, George Wiebe, and William Baerg, as well as world-famous singers like Edith Wiens.

Not long before his death, Robert Shaw, the renowned chorale leader, told of his love affair with the Mennonite choral tradition. On one occasion in the early 1980s he asked George Wiebe, longtime music director at Canadian Mennonite Bible College, "When are you going to invite me to Winnipeg?" Shaw ended up making three visits to Winnipeg to conduct the Mennonite Festival Chorus.

Mennonites have distinguished themselves across the musical landscape. They perform in symphony orchestras from Edmonton to St. Louis. They have produced prominent composers like Larry Warkentin and Randolph Peters, and instrumentalists like Irmgard Baerg (piano/harpsichord) and Eugene Friesen (cello). Ben Heppner, one of the top operatic tenors in the world, descends from Russian Mennonite stock.

There is even a "Mennonite Piano Concerto," written by Victor Davies using beloved Mennonite hymn tunes. Recorded by the London Symphony Orchestra, it serves as the sound track for the Russian Mennonite motion picture, *And When They Shall Ask.*

Writing the vision

The Russian Mennonites' literary tradition is relatively young. As far back as Polish-Prussia, their home libraries were limited to the Bible and the *Martyrs' Mirror*. In Russia they seldom moved beyond immediate practical needs like devotional material and recent history.

Their multilingual background didn't help. In which language should writers write and publishers publish? High German, the language of worship, which replaced Dutch during the sojourn in Polish-Prussia? Low German, the folk language of the back yard? Or English, the new language of daily commerce? Today, the answer is simpler, as fewer and fewer Mennonites speak Low German, and only new immigrants speak German.

When Russian Mennonites reached the stage of seasoned reflection, they first needed to share the poignant

No Russian Mennonite has received more literary acclaim than novelist Rudy Wiebe, one of Canada's leading writers. A few of his books are shown here.

memoirs of terror. The tribulation of the 1920s Mennonites, who endured suffering not matched since the martyrdom of 16th-century Anabaptism, was regarded as their own holocaust, and people were determined to preserve their memories, at least for their families if not for a larger readership.

Among the early published writers in Manitoba was Arnold Dyck, perhaps best known for his Low German skits that poked fun at Mennonite foibles. At a different place in the spectrum were writers whose spiritually uplifting material remained specifically devotional. Yet another genre has been poems, novels, and short stories by writers no longer in the faith tradition but who creatively process their own pain of departure from it. One of the earliest of this genre was *Flamethrowers* (possibly the first

In 2000, after more than half a century of running their own educational programs, the Mennonite Brethren and General Conference Mennonites (now Mennonite Church Canada) of central Canada merged their colleges to form Canadian Mennonite University in Winnipeg, Manitoba.

Mennonite novel written in English) by Oklahoma newspaper reporter Gordon Friesen (1936).

In Kansas, Katie Funk Wiebe has been a distinguished author of columns, essays, and books that interpret the Mennonite pilgrimage in a modern world. Esther Loewen Vogt became beloved as writer of pioneer stories for children.

Until recent decades, few Russian Mennonite writers have managed to freely engage great themes outside their ethnic tradition. Of those who have, some of the more prominent include poets Jean Janzen, Elmer Suderman, Sarah Klassen, and David Waltner-Toews. Novelist Rudy Wiebe, one of Canada's top writers, has twice won his country's Governor General's Award for Literature.

Education

Since 1977 the University of Winnipeg has had a Chair of Mennonite Studies. Both of its occupants have been Russian Mennonites. In 1989 Menno Simons College (MSC) was formed at the same university. In 2000 MSC, along with Concord College and Canadian Mennonite Bible College (both of which had long ties with local universities allowing them to offer accredited programs), formed Canadian Mennonite University. Russian Mennonite professors also populate the ranks of major universities from the University of British Columbia and Stanford on one coast, to Harvard and Yale on the other.

Business

Drive along the Trans-Canada Highway and see semi-trailer rigs with names like Reimer, Penner, and Kindersley, all major trucking firms founded by Russian Mennonites. Turn on the radio or TV and hear ads declaring, "It's worth the trip to Steinbach," where Mennonite automobile dealers have made this southeastern Manitoba community into "the automobile city." Canadian readers waiting breathlessly for the latest installment by their favorite bestselling author will likely buy a book that rolled off the press of the Friesen company in Altona, Manitoba, one of Canada's leading printers. Buy peaches from Ontario, sunflower seeds from Manitoba, potato chips from Alberta, hydroponic tomatoes from British Columbia, raisins from California, wheat from Kansas, or corn from South Dakota, and benefit from the output of farmers with Russian Mennonite background.

The Mennonite Heritage Centre on the Canadian Mennonite University campus in Winnipeg, Manitoba, provides a home for archival records, historical research, and a gallery for Mennonite artists.

Frank Peters
Building

Frank C. Peters, a former president of Wilfrid Laurier University in Waterloo, Ontario, was one of many Russian Mennonites to serve with distinction in higher education.

Entertainment and politics

Tune in to the Canadian Broadcasting Corporation (CBC), Canada's cross-country radio network, and hear the warm tones of Howard Dyck or Eric Friesen, both of whom learned their craft at a modest, Mennonite-owned station in Altona.

Russian Mennonites have participated in major team sports—professional hockey, football (both NFL and CFL), and baseball. Olympic bronze medal speed skater Cindy Klassen belongs to a Canadian congregation of Russian Mennonites.

Numerous Mennonites have done well in politics, from state representatives in Kansas to provincial cabinets in Canada. Jake Epp, son of a Mennonite minister from the Molotschna Colony, served in Canada's Parliament for more than 20 years, including a long term as Minister of Health. Gordon Thiessen, grandson of a Mennonite minister from Saskatchewan, was Governor of the Bank of Canada, the country's leading financial officer. Many Mennonites have been awarded the Order of Canada, the country's highest civilian recognition.

Few areas of endeavor have not been touched by descendants of Russian Mennonites.

Epilogue

In the beginning of this story about Mennonites from Russia, geography played an important part. Today physical location isn't nearly as important to the Mennonite profile. It is unlikely that mass migration will ever again figure so prominently in the Mennonite story. After all, there are few, if any, geographical frontiers left.

Fewer first-generation Russian Mennonites can be found in Canada and the United States. The last of those who were part of the major migrations to North America are getting on in years.

Their descendants still journey back to the "homeland" to glimpse their past. They visit the original villages (virtually all since renamed), pay tribute in cemeteries, and photograph the old buildings. (Many of them are gone or crumbling, but some are still remarkably intact and in continued use.) These curious children savor the scent of idyllic times, when Great-Grandpa was a contented farmer and Grandma frolicked as a child among chestnut trees.

Perhaps they replay the grief of loss, the horror of families executed by bandits. They may muse before a stately brick church, two stories high with Gothic windows and clay roof tiles, and ponder the pulse of corporate worship. Maybe they still hear, in the breezes of nostalgia, the tones of Mennonite preachers holding forth with words of nurture and instruction, as well as rebuke.

The migratory genes that drew Mennonites from Europe to Russia, and to all the Americas and beyond, seem to have found a measure of rest. For the Russian Mennonites, as for many of the million other Anabaptists in the worldwide communion, today's geography is more spiritual, a landscape of the soul.

Different kinds of homelands are being occupied as Mennonites tread fresh paths of diversity, embrace new brothers and sisters around the globe, and reweave the strands that bind together this remarkable people, the Mennonites.

Readings and Sources

Dyck, Cornelius J., editor
1967   *An Introduction to Mennonite History.* Scottdale, Pa.: Herald Press.
        A popular, readable history of Anabaptism's European beginnings to Russia, North America, Asia, Africa, and Latin America.

Epp, Frank H.
1962   *Mennonite Exodus.* Altona, Man.: D.W. Friesen & Sons.
        A detailed depiction of the rescue and resettlement of an uprooted people following the Communist Revolution.

1974   *Mennonites in Canada, 1786-1920: The History of a Separate People.* Toronto: Macmillan.
        An analysis of several strands of Mennonites and their efforts to maintain identity amid relentless pressure to assimilate.

1982   *Mennonites in Canada, 1920-1940: A People's Struggle for Survival.* Toronto: Macmillan.
        Between the two world wars, Mennonites battle for separate schools, migrate to Latin America, and deal with a new influx of Mennonites from Russia.

Friesen, Rudy P. with Sergey Shmakin
1996 *Into the Past: Buildings of the Mennonite Common-wealth.* Winnipeg, Man.: Raduga Publications.
A Mennonite architect provides a visual tour of hundreds of homes, schools, churches, and factories (many still standing) erected by Mennonites in the 19th and early 20th centuries.

Juhnke, James C.
1975 *A People of Two Kingdoms: The Political Accultura-tion of the Kansas Mennonites.* Newton, Kan.: Faith and Life Press.
A close-up look at an immigrant community's adjustment to the strange, new face of America they found upon arriving on the plains of Kansas.

Loewen, Harry and Steven Nolt
1996 *Through Fire & Water: An Overview of Mennonite History.* Scottdale, Pa.: Herald Press.
This popular-level book, rich with biographical sketches, illustrations, anecdotes, and cartoons, places the Anabaptist drama in continuity with the first-century Christian church.

Neufeld, Dietrich, translated and edited by Al Reimer
1980 *A Russian Dance of Death: Revolution and Civil War in the Ukraine.* Winnipeg, Man.: Hyperion; Scottdale, Pa.: Herald Press.
A translated journal relates stories of murder and plunder amid the brutality and horror of the Russian Revolution.

Regehr, T. D.

1996 *Mennonites in Canada, 1939-1970: A People Transformed.* Toronto: University of Toronto Press.

An immigrant group moves from village to city, enters business and the professions, and adopts new values that sometimes clash with their past.

Rempel, John D. and Paul Tiessen, editors

1981 *Forever Summer, Forever Sunday: Peter Gerhard Rempel's Photographs of Mennonites in Russia, 1890-1917.* St. Jacobs, Ont.: Sand Hills Books.

Early photographs present a penetrating view of the Russian Mennonite golden age on the eve of its imminent destruction.

Smith, C. Henry

1950 *The Story of the Mennonites.* Newton, Kan.: Mennonite Publication Office.

Though dated, this classic provides a sweeping overview of the Mennonite pilgrimage.

Stoesz, Edgar and Muriel T. Stackley

1999 *Garden in the Wilderness.* Winnipeg, Man.: CMBC Publications.

A recent look at how Russian Mennonite immigrants found refuge in Paraguay and transformed their surroundings.

Toews, J. B.
1995   *JB: The Autobiography of a Twentieth-Century Mennonite Pilgrim.* Fresno, Calif.: Center for MB Studies.

Memoirs of a vigilant observer of the Russian Mennonite experience through most of the 20th century.

Toews, Paul
1996   *Mennonites in American Society, 1930-1970: Modernity and the Persistence of Religious Community.* Scottdale, Pa.: Herald Press.

The fourth and final volume of the Mennonite Experience in America series examines how Mennonite identity fared through four tumultuous decades of American life.

Urry, James
1989   *None But Saints: The Transformation of Mennonite Life in Russia 1789-1889.* Winnipeg, Man.: Hyperion Press.

A New Zealand anthropologist probes the dynamics of economic, social, political, and religious change during the Mennonites' first century in Russia.

Fiction

Birdsell, Sandra

2001   *The Russlaender.* Toronto: McClelland & Stewart.
A poignant, best-selling account of a Mennonite family fleeing the violence of the Russian Revolution and beginning a new life on the Canadian Prairies.

Martens, Wilfred

1980   *River of Glass.* Scottdale, Pa.: Herald Press.
The dramatic story of Mennonites who escaped the tightening grip of Russian Communism by fleeing to China, and experienced painful lessons of self-discovery along the way.

Wiebe, Rudy

1962   *Peace Shall Destroy Many.* Toronto: McClelland & Stewart.
In his first book Canada's leading Mennonite novelist explores life and contradictions in a small Mennonite community during World War II.

1970   *The Blue Mountains of China.* Grand Rapids: Eerdmans.
A saga of Russian Mennonite families who scatter around the world seeking their own version of a promised land.

2001   *Sweeter Than All The World.* Toronto: Alfred A. Knopf.
This voyage of discovery and redemption follows the tumultuous Russian Mennonite story over five centuries.

About the Author

Wally Kroeker grew up in southern Manitoba with one foot on the farm and one in the city. He descends from two different streams of Russian Mennonites. His paternal ancestors emigrated from the Chortitza Colony to southern Manitoba in 1876. His mother migrated as a child from the Molotschna Colony in 1925.

He has spent more than 35 years as a reporter and editor, specializing in business and religion. He began his career with the *Regina Leader-Post* and later served as editor of the *Saskatchewan Business Journal* and as business writer and assistant city editor of the *Winnipeg Tribune.* He was assistant editor of *Moody Monthly* (Chicago) and for 10 years was editor of *The Christian Leader,* the magazine of the U.S. Mennonite Brethren Church.

Since 1985 Kroeker has been director of publications for Mennonite Economic Development Associates (MEDA) and editor of its magazine, *The Marketplace.*

His freelance articles have appeared in nearly a hundred business and religious publications. He is author of *God's Week has Seven Days* (Herald) and co-author of *Faith Dilemmas for Marketplace Christians* (Herald).

Kroeker studied journalism at Northwestern University in Chicago and completed his undergraduate degree in religious studies at Tabor College, Hillsboro, Kansas. He has a master of arts degree in theology from the Mennonite Brethren Biblical Seminary, Fresno, Calif.

He and his wife Millie, who teaches English as a Second Language, attend River East Mennonite Brethren Church in Winnipeg. They have two sons, Scott and Joel.

Kroeker considers himself a global Anabaptist and an enthusiastic supporter of the Mennonite World Conference. He has visited Anabaptists in Russia, Ukraine, Germany, France, India, Tanzania, Mozambique, Zimbabwe, Mexico, Bolivia, and Paraguay.

His hobbies include following Major League Baseball, cooking five-alarm chili, and doting on his three grandchildren.